Love, Life, God:

The Journey of Creation

Also by Jarrad Hewett

The Big E: Everything is Energy

Unleashing the Power of Everyday Wisdom

Love, Life, God:

The Journey of Creation

By Jarrad Hewett

Legacy Publications First Edition - September 2010

This book is dedicated to friends, family, and shaumbra: past, present, and future.

You've touched my life in so many countless ways.

I'm truly grateful for your unending love and support and honored to have shared creation with you.

Table of Contents

Preface

"You will write."

I was in a Barnes and Noble with two of my friends, in the checkout line, when I heard this affirmation.

I had heard these words before, but they were more like thoughts in my head. This time, however, the voice wasn't coming from inside. I turned to see if anybody was talking to me. For a moment, it seemed like time was standing still, until one of my friends snapped her fingers.

"Hey, Spacey McSpacerton, the cashier's open. Let's move it."

I only had a couple of moments to process what had just occurred, but in all honesty, it wasn't really that out of the ordinary for me. In fact, I was kind of excited. I had been working with a group of healers for several years, and I had spent the past year or so teaching workshops on moving and directing energy. The building blocks of what is presented in this book had already begun to trickle into my consciousness, and my entire existence had been greatly altered as a result.

This breakthrough was a long time in coming. From childhood, I had experienced dreams that would ultimately come to pass—a gift that paid off quite nicely one spring break at the roulette table. From time to time, I also saw (and was pretty darn scared of) non-physical beings or spirits. As a matter of fact, I ignored that aspect of who I was almost up until my early twenties. But, as I opened up to the idea that everything was energy, the fears began to subside and the answers to the questions I'd been asking began to come. As I learned to communicate with and direct my own energy, or balance certain beliefs and fears that kept me in certain patterns of sickness, lack, and limitation, more and more "strange" and miraculous things began to happen: One of which was the awareness and ability to communicate with those who had physically passed on from this plane.

The first "other" energy I remember seeing was my grandpa. I don't have a whole lot of memories of him from when he was alive, and I was so shocked and freaked out when he showed up in my bedroom that I honestly don't remember much about the experience other than frantically calling a healer friend afterward.

"Hey . . . I just saw my grandpa."

"Oh, great. How is he?" she asked.

"Dead."

"Oh. Well, did you ask him what he wanted?"

Did I ask him what he wanted? I was raised a strict Southern Baptist. Despite some of the "strange" occurrences in my life, I still thought that after death you either went to heaven, or you went to hell. This guy had been dead *for almost twenty years*, and now he was standing in my bedroom smiling at me. Apparently, unlike me, my friend didn't have a problem with this.

A few weeks later, the cousin of another friend of mine came through. I called her with some trepidation—not even knowing if she had a dead cousin. I described what he was wearing (a dated brown suit, his shirt, hat, etc), and she started crying.

"That's my cousin all right. I have a picture of the two of us in my nightstand. It was taken at my Grandma's funeral, and he's wearing exactly what you just described. That was the last time I ever saw him alive."

As I started to open up to the "reality" of what I was experiencing, more and more "strange" things began happening.

At a workshop one day, a girl began crying hysterically. She explained that three of her relatives were missing in a snowstorm in Oregon. They had been missing for four days, and rescue workers were beginning to fear the worst. My healing partners and I sat down and had the group focus. Suddenly, I felt something in me expand outward. I was still in my body, but I was simultaneously so much bigger. I didn't understand what was happening at the time, but I was tapping into "the field"—the one universal energy. I then saw a highway sign and a mile marker. I told the girl they were fine, and that they would be found. The next morning, I received an email. They had found the family exactly where I had said.

Holy. Crap.

I felt validated and scared out of my mind all at the same time.

Over the next few months, I received constant validations. For a while, I thought communicating with the dead or helping find lost loved ones was to be my spiritual calling. I hadn't yet realized that I was creating these experiences through my own desire to expand my consciousness. Plainly put, this was all just another aspect of my totality that was unfolding. I was tapping into the infiniteness of who I AM.

What had begun as a sort of "peering through the veil" wound up as the realization that the veil—all veils—was just an illusion. There is no separation. As I began to remember who I really was and to open up to all that I AM, I had even greater experiences of Oneness.

Don't get me wrong. I spent a lot of time ignoring all of this and trying to pretend it wasn't really happening, but as I opened up to it, I began opening up to the greater me. My life began to change in extraordinary ways. Miracles began happening all around me. One moment, I would be standing in a grocery store, and the next, I would be looking *through* the store and out into a vast Universe of beings and potential.

"What in the world is all of this?" I began to wonder.

Then, one day, came an audible answer.

Introduction

The Big Fat Giant Whole

Most stories start with a beginning such as: "Once Upon a Time," "When I was younger," or "When I was born." I'm sure you're thinking that you too had a starting point, a finite beginning. We're here to tell you that you did not. You have always been, and you have always been perfect. Life after life, you've manifested what must seem like infinite "beginnings" when in fact, you never began from scratch. You simply always were. What we are asking you to do is to give up the idea of any beginning, and thus give up the story of you.

What does that mean, "give up the story of you?"

It's like the old saying goes, "If you want something you've never had, you've got to do something you've never done." In this case, it involves examining who and what you are and realizing that you are not the sum of your past. The future is yours to create. If you want to be a new you, be a new you – but know that you can't make anything totally new by using parts from the old. In simpler terms, we're going to show you how to forgive and how to truly love.

Wow.

It's quite a journey, but it's definitely one you won't regret taking. Now, some people may lose their bearings a bit as we go, and to them we want to say that's not a bad thing; in fact, it's a blessing. It's the first step in waking up and truly seeing yourself as God sees you. Right side up is just a perspective.

All we'll ask is for everyone to be present - to be in the moment of now - and to really allow themselves to express, experience, and feel the words that we say.

You keep saying, "we." I think I already know the answer to this, but can you explain who "you" are?

"We" are also really an "I," but we'll get to that later. For now, a good answer for that question might be to simply say: "We are the collective whole, or Source Energy - the consciousness of All That Is - moving forward on our journey of expansion and celebration."

We're coming forward through our conversation with you, so that all may know from whence they are, because again, none came; all have simply been. We are frequency. We are vibration. We are thought. We are creation. We are you. We are All That Is.

How was that?

That was good. I like it. But that just raises another question.

Which is?

Why have you come forward now?

We've come forward now to help show you and everyone reading these words their Oneness with Source - that which most people have called God and have placed outside of themselves. Simply put, We've come so that you may know.

Know what?

All That is.

That sounds like a lofty goal, even for Source.

Indeed it is, yet the goal has already been reached. All that you are - all that you ever were - is infinite, and within the realm of infinity, we are all complete.

Now, you think that you know who you are. You are an individual. To some extent, yes; you are. However, you are an individualized expression of Source energy - which we all are. We've come forward now to help you understand that while you perceive yourself on this grand journey - a journey you are very much on - you needn't take it so seriously. You needn't ever feel alone, and you needn't ever suffer. You are greatly, greatly loved by all that is, because you are all that is, and all that is, is always complete. Got it?

Got it!

We'd like to add that even though you're having the experience of this conversation, there really isn't any separation between us – just as there really isn't separation between anything. Scientifically, you know that if you look at anything under a high enough powered microscope, you'll see space. Space isn't separation; it's actually unity. Everything exists in this space: you, the world, the heavens, every one and every thing.

That's pretty cool.

It really is. It's also quite vast. Think about it. If there is no separation, you're never really in what you just called a mono-logue. "Mono," infers a singularity of or separation of being, and this -

among other notions - is what we're here to shed some light on.

Awesome. Well, where would you like to start?

(Laughs) Why, at the "beginning," of course. You just received a text message from your friend. What did it say?

He was asking me to check out an engagement ring online that he is looking at for his girlfriend ... That's the beginning?

Yes, and no. We told you, there is no beginning. But, to fully illustrate our point, we'll explain the nature of things using terms you're familiar with.

Well, that text was about relationships. Is that where we're starting?

Yes, indeed. We wish to begin by exploring your relationship to yourself.

Why did you have me type "your Self," "your self," and then "yourself?"

We wished to show you the degree of separation that exists in your thinking even now within the Oneness of You. For you are all there is, and if you are separate from yourself, how can you serve as the All that you are?

Okay, now <u>that's</u> confusing. Can you break it down for me, in plain English?

That which you call God, has always existed. If we call it energy, you can understand it in a more detached, yet specific way. Energy is neither created nor destroyed. All that is, has always been. It simply manifests in ever-changing ways. Thus is the story of you.

You mean like past lives and stuff?

Exactly: past lives . . . and STUFF! The "stuff" is the part we wish to explore right now. Within the "Stuff"—which is you by the way, it's all you—lies every single dimension, every single probability, every single animation of being ness and it's corresponding stillness and void.

So you're telling me at my core, I'm basically a big fat giant whole?

Yes. You are nothing. You are no thing. You are every thing and everything. You are all that is.

Well, if I'm everything, why is there war? Why is there poverty? Heck, why am I even here?

The answer to that question lies within your degree of Self-Love. But we don't want to get ahead of our-self right now. Do you see what you just did?

Got ahead of myself?

No. You wrote "our-self!" You're already starting to get it. Impressive.

Chapter One

Who are you?

As we have said, to understand that there is no beginning, you've got to understand that there is no question of who you are. You are, as was so eloquently put by the Buddha, the result of all that you have thought. The Bible tells us something of the same, "As a man thinketh in his heart, so is he." So ask yourself, "What are my thoughts? Where do they come from? Just what, who, and how am I?"

We'll help you out by giving you the answer: You are unlimited thought. You are infinite vibration. You are energy within a field viewing itself as a connected individualization of Source.

Think of it this way: when God moved upon the waters . . .

Whoa. Really? We're going Biblical?

This is an allusion to the "illusion" of how you think you came into being. Rather, how you came to find yourself defining yourself as an individualized self, free of any innate connection to creation or that which you call God.

Okay. Sorry. Continue.

No. That was it. "God moved upon the waters." What are you?

...Water?

Yep, mostly water.

So the phrase: "God moved upon the face of the water" is really the creation story in one sentence?

Nope. It's the creation story of your individualized self. You are the energy that moved upon the waters. You are the energy that created your individualization.

Why would I do that? Why would I consciously choose to say to God, "Hey, peace out. I'm going to go do my own thing for a while?" That doesn't make much sense to me.

We'll get there. You are the energy of God – Creation - made manifest in human form. And you've been here many times, by the way.

(Pause)

Now might be a good time to take a break.

But this is just getting good!

You've moved into a place of resistance and your mind is starting to cloud things up a bit. We need you to be clear. Take a break. You won't lose your place, we promise.

(I was asked to return to the computer the following day.)

We've asked you to come back in tonight so that we can address the point of your creation.

Me as God moving on the water?

Right. You moved upon the water, became the water - realizing that this is not water as you know it - and burst into form.

Well, I didn't literally burst upon the scene. I had a good eight months of gestation.

This gives you a little more insight into what we call water. We don't want to get too much into the physical act of pro-creation, however, know that <u>you</u> are the one who moved upon the waters.

Why did you have me hyphenate "procreation?"

Because whether you consciously perceive it is as such, all creation is pro-active. All creation is a further exploration of All That Is. You are both the explorer and the explored. You create you. In this life, on this plane, there was a physical act of procreation, but that act didn't create you. The participants of that act didn't create you. You created you.

Wait. Are you saying I created me? ...So what? My parents were just kind of like two random participants who got together to bring me forth?

No. You brought you forth. Your parents were chosen, by you, with their consent. Remember, you're perfect just as you are. You don't need to DO anything. You make your birthing agreements - which sometimes differ from your family agreements - far in advance.

Not to backtrack too much, but I thought I began as I moved upon the waters?

In so much as anyone "began," that's true. What we're talking about now is specific to choosing an incarnate lifetime on this planet. You chose the vessels to provide the genetic kindling - if you will. Source/You then came in with the spark and made fire. You made life where only chemical codes existed. You moved upon the "water" and began programming yourself in the womb.

Interesting. This brings up the question of "When does life exist?"

You're missing the point. Life - your life - always exists. There is no point of origin for something that has always been. We know what you're asking in this perspective, and we can offer you this in response: as the physical aspect of that which is to become you - that is to say, the body you will create for physical experience - begins to form, you are present both inside and outside of its existence, much as you are now.

What do you mean as I am now?

One question at a time. You're an omnipresent being - you always have been. As Source Energy, you're connected to everything that is—which is all that has ever been and all that will ever be. Cool, huh?

You seem to have just gotten excited.

Oh yes. We are very excited. Excitement is a wonderful vibration. You yourself should try it more often.

Hey. That was a cheap shot.

We're just messing with you to show you that God has a sense of humor. Now, as we were saying, you're omnipresent and omnipotent.

Wait. I'm all-knowing also?

Of course. You've chosen an individualized experience of Oneness wherein you identify yourself mostly with the personality you are now - and we say mostly because in cases such as yours, some people awaken to their multidimensional, past-life selves in a way they often times find hard to communicate. You've chosen to come here and commit to this reality. You commit only because you don't always remember that you don't have to forget. You're safe at all times, and at any time in this life, you may choose to "un-commit" and remember all that you are. In this remembering, is the being.

So, let me see if I got all of that. You're saying life doesn't start at conception because life never actually starts. I was in existence in some form or another (which I hear we'll be talking about later) before choosing - and it is important to know that I CHOSE - to come into this physical existence in this body. You're also saying that I had a hand in programming my physical attributes.

Yes and more than a hand. You were the architect of your own design.

Ummm ... Okay, so at what point did I focus all of my energy or beingness into, or onto this plane?

At no point. You're still very much alive, as you would call it, in other places of time and space - at which point we feel it necessary to add that what you perceive as time doesn't exist. As man so humbly channeled in the past, "I am the Alpha and Omega." To the One Energy, all - including elements of time and space - are one.

Whoa. That's a little difficult to . . .

(At this point, the phone rang and I became distracted.)

Pulled you out, didn't it?

Yeah. It did. I kinda feel like I need a break. Is that okay?

Of course. We'll finish when you return.

(I returned the following evening)

A bit more in the present tonight?

Yeah. I think so. I kind of drifted away at the end of yesterday's chat.

That goes perfectly with what we were speaking about. At any given moment - which is always the present – you're literally capable of experiencing any "other" moment there is, because there is no separation of time or space - of anything for that matter.

Can you explain that?

Well, you like to refer to the picture of the clock that we gave you. Only, until now, your understanding of that picture was limited. As you believe, the clock represents the One Energy - The All That Is. In the very middle of the clock face, as you understand it, is your soul or the You behind the you.

The various numbers of time mark literal destinations in what you believe is a time/space continuum. The hour hand then is the literal focus of your soul into a specific being in a specific time/space reality/identity, while the minute hand may be used to identify the different potentials that you will either choose to fulfill or use to birth new desires that exist within the context of or relation to the hour hand. However, this clock would have many hands branching out from its center pointing to many different numbers—all of which you understand to be different lifetimes—that which you previously understood as past or future lifetimes.

I think I'm losing the "whole" picture.

Well, just as one pixel can be viewed as a whole or combined with others to make up a bigger picture, so can Source. All of the pixels come together and form the whole, but like with a hologram, the Source coding is whole within each unit. In other words, all of these tiny pieces have the whole within them. The you that you know in this existence is one of these many pixels, and you fit together with the rest of Source to make up the whole—and, that whole is already within you. So with regard to the pixels and hour hands, all of these lifetimes are yours, but you are currently focused on only one.

You mean consciously and according to my belief, right?

Yes.

Okay, so basically, all time exists simultaneously, and that while my soul - if we can call it that ...

We can, but know that you and your Soul are one. It's not some menacing overlord whom you are programmed to serve, nor is it some greater being. It's you. You just perceive yourself in a way that implies separation.

So then, my soul isn't focused on one reality, it's my perception?

We're getting there. But, if we may interrupt your thought process and continue exploring our examples of the clock and pixels, we would like to move further into the understanding that no separation exists "between" anything - whether it be lifetimes or people.

I'm sensing a big theme.

Yes, and it is important for you to understand just how all encompassing this is. The clock represents all energy. We used the picture of a clock because you associate it with time. However, within the one energy, where all time exists, it exists not as time, but as the expansion of the present moment.

I'm not quite with you on that one.

Stay with us. Don't drift. Your perception of the hour hand was correct in that it represents you, but it represents *the "you"* within the mass consciousness. It represents the part of you that while it is the all, has come forth to experience singularity—springing forth from Source into this embodiment. Yet, you've come in to this moment simply by being what you already are. This part of you perceives a passage of time, but in fact, you are timeless. Your orientation to Source doesn't change. This would appear to you then as the hand remaining in the same place while the clock face, representing Source, spins. In actuality, what you call your soul is Source Energy, and as such it is experiencing itself in an infinite way. This means, according to your picture, there are an infinite number of hour hands, and the clock is always expanding according to Source Energy's desire for new experience. Do you follow?

My brain gets it: "There is no time," but I feel like my being doesn't quite get it.

You're separating again. Your being gets it. You - in all of your physicality - are the physical manifestation of spirit. You are not IN your body. You are experiencing all of you. Your body and spirit are in direct relation: the body is the physical expression of your spirit—of your energy.

I don't know what happened, but I think I just got it.

You integrated, and the resistance to knowing left. Good riddance.

Wow. Okay, so let me see if I can recap this. I am Source Energy.

You could really stop there.

Okay, but I want to understand how this all comes together. So, I am Source Energy, manifesting as me. While I am consciously experiencing this life...

Oh, you're consciously experiencing all life. You don't get that yet, but you will.

Ahem!

Sorry.

While I'm consciously experiencing myself in this reality, what I believed to be past lives, also exist at the same moment?

Yes. What you would term "future" lives as well.

Okay, so all of these lifetimes are happening energetically at the same time?

Yes. You've just made a breakthrough. You said "energetically." You see, EVERYTHING is energy: you, your desk, your computer, your mother, your father, and the trees outside - everything. Your perception of you is that you are in fact you - a solid being with some squishy parts who believes he has an identity that makes him a unique and separate individual. In fact, your uniqueness, your ego if you will, is just the mechanism that allows the illusion of separation to play out.

I feel like I've heard this explanation before.

You probably have. We've been implying this all along. So then, energy simply is. You've taken this energy, which is you, and said that you wish to experience it in a new way. Think of this lifetime as a ride at a water park. You have eagerly climbed to the top of the slide, knowing all along that once you experience the slide, you will be back in the pool, safe and sound.

What if I don't like water?

It's a metaphor. Go with it.

You excitedly climb to the top and shoot down the slide. The slide is your life experience. You can embrace it, fear it, love it, or even change it - because while you're on the slide, you are also engineering it.

Kind of like a choose-your-own adventure book, but on a larger, physical scale?

Precisely. The slide is whatever form you wish it to be, and when you're finished with what you've chosen to experience, you arrive back in the pool, where you can float about, get out and use the restroom, or climb back up the slide and do it all over again.

All of this while staying in the moment?

We'll add another element or two here. You're not only experiencing the water park, you're not only creating the ride as you experience it, but you're also the entire water park. The entirety of the situation is you. The slide is an element of you. The you who is experiencing the ride is an element of you. The creator of the ride is you. The eager parent waiting at the base of the ride is you. It's all you.

You're saying I'm safe, huh?

Completely. Even if you create an enclosed slide and you become disoriented to the point of not knowing which way is up or down, you're still safe. Just because you are momentarily afraid of your own creation, doesn't mean you aren't safe. You think that no one makes it out of life alive; when in fact, that's not the point. You're always alive. You just finish the ride.

Now that we have covered a few of the basics...

Basics? That all seemed fairly complex and mind blowing to me.

(Excitedly) Oh, This is just the beginning.

Well how much more expansive are we going to get?

Let's just say, you might want to strap yourself in.

Chapter Two

My Creation

Everything in your world is a form of energy. You view it as objects with perceivable motion. By this we mean that when most hear the word energy, they think of atoms and basic particles, when in fact it's more than what you would call solid matter that is energy. It is also what you think you cannot perceive like thoughts, impulses, and reactions.

Can you explain what you mean by saying reactions are energy?

Certainly. Think of it as a wave. A wave comes into your field - what we'll call your known presence for now - and it washes over you. In a totally balanced energy field, nothing is affected. However, where fear is present, this energy wave will ignite within the hosting field any and all shared fears. Thus, this wave is perceived by your energy as a foreign invader, the energetic equivalent of a bacterium being introduced into a healthy body. The immune cells go into attack mode to neutralize the perceived threat. So then, your energetic body, which makes up your physical body but also extends out from your physical body, may perceive itself as under attack.

Maybe we're thinking of two different things. I was thinking of something like an allergic reaction.

Perfect. The same principal applies. Something your body perceives as foreign comes in, and your body goes into fight mode. All of this is energy-transfer. This is a physical example of what happens in the other planes of existence.

I'm not sure how we got from creation to reaction.

Well, we want to start here to move the consciousness out of reaction so that it can create from choice. Reaction is not choice; it is a conditioned response.

Okay, so explain then what you meant by: "This is a physical example of what happens in the other planes."

Gladly. We'll use the example of a party. You are very familiar with this example, are you not? You walk into a room and as you move about, you pick up feelings. You may see someone who makes you smile. You may become excited to see someone else, or you may see a person and get that "stay away" vibe. Well, those "vibes" are what we are talking about. The awareness of physical beings expands out from their inner being. There is a subtle energy system that surrounds everyone.

Like chakras?

More like a glow. You know it as an aura, but it is much more complex than you could imagine. Within this energy field is a type of sonar that spreads out ahead of your physical consciousness and "feels out" the room. Some people are aware of this system, some are not. The awareness is not the point.

It's not?

No. Because *it is*, whether you know it consciously or not, a part of who you are and you use it at all times. Now, sometimes when the energy fields begin to interact and play together, fear lights up in your system. Physically, this can look like anything from a simple feeling of unease to an all-out panic or hysteria.

That's intense. The way you describe it, I think I might be better off just staying home and having people slip me takeout through the mail slot.

Well, that's one option. But you see it is not necessarily their energy that has provoked this reaction. In your state of unknowing, you simply forgot that you are your own creator, and you began to fear something. This fear then caused you to give your creatorship away in that you allowed another to create.

But I thought we were all one?

Indeed we are. However, you are also individualized expressions with your own desires. In this scenario, your fear has weakened your vibrations and you have allowed creation based on these fears.

Wow. So, can you illustrate this with a story?

Absolutely. Say you go on a job interview. While sitting in the lobby waiting, you suddenly begin to feel uneasy. Now, you say to yourself, "This is stupid. What am I worried about? I'm prepared, and I'm the best candidate for this job."

I'm having wicked déjà vu right now.

Yes. We will discuss that in a later chapter, but for now we will say this: While you create in the moment of now, occasionally, you like to take trips down the trail of possible outcomes. You were deciding in your sleep what venture you wanted to tackle next, and you chose to play with your "linear existence" by following certain choices to their probable outcomes. We'll talk more about this later, we promise. But for now, we want to finish our story.

Please.

So you begin to feel uneasy, and you don't know why. You look over and see another candidate wearing a suit that is much nicer than yours. Suddenly, you feel like maybe he will make a better impression than you. In this scenario, his confidence ignited within your field of energy a fear around confidence - whether that is a fear of being overconfident, not confident enough, or any variation in between. Keep in mind, this is a very simple explanation, yet it will suffice for our purpose.

So what do I do then to keep that from happening?

You claim Self-Love.

Self-Love? That's all?

It's more powerful than you can imagine. We simply want you to state, "I Am Self-Love." The answers to your questions are already known to your consciousness, and for now we wish for you to work with us on an unconscious level. Trust us. The information is there. We will explain what this direction of energy does, but for now, we ask for your trust and know that Self-Love is the blueprint for all creation.

Okay. Can I ask what claiming self love does?

Certainly. It frees your energy for choice.

But I thought you said we were always at choice.

You are; it's all about choice. Let's say you've chosen to ask for a million dollars, yet you've also chosen not to bring that into your experience (In other words, you've asked for a million dollars, but you didn't receive a million dollars). You see, you're choosing to ask, and on some level. You're also choosing not to receive.

That's jacked up! So I'm receiving based on my choices - which includes the choice to allow?

Indeed.

Why on earth wouldn't I choose to allow what I want?

You have consciously chosen as much as you can consciously choose. Beneath your conscious direction, however, has been reaction—which has kept you in the cycle of recreation, rather than creation.

So my reactions or fears have actually served to keep me in the same box I'm consciously asking to move out of?

Yes. But don't think of your situation as a box to escape from. The need to "escape" will only keep recreating the thing you are trying to escape from because the focus will be on escaping – which is a reaction.

Wow. You know, I'm starting to realize that I don't just react to other people's energy; I react to my own.

Precisely. And in fact, what you think of as a reaction to another's energy is in fact a reaction to your own.

Because I'm separating again?

Yep, and no one has the power to create for you except you. What you are reacting to is the part of your own energy whose self-creation you have given away.

Given away?

Yes. To someone else, to some other idea, to a limited belief, to fear, or to a power you perceive as outside of yourself: economic conditions, for instance. The beautiful thing is, this energy is yours. You don't even have to reclaim it because it never really went anywhere. It was just your perception. Claim that, and direct it.

By claiming I Am Self-Love?

Yes! Now, once you move out of reaction, you are ready to decide. The decision you must make is "Do I stay in conscious creation, or do I move back into reaction? Do I maintain the illusion that I'm a victim, or do I move into the power of knowing I am my own creator?"Check in with yourself and ask, "Am I creating from a place of love, joy, and freedom, or am I coming from a limited perspective?"

Okay, well I definitely claim Self-Love around that. Now what?

Now you have moved into what we call conscious creation. You are no longer wasting energy by reacting. You are now directing your energy in a balanced way via choice.

So, how does all of this relate to re-creation vs. creation?

Think of it in terms of "back-story."

Like in the movies?

Yes. Sometimes people come into this life with a reactionary energy. Meaning, they're still creating, but they're creating from a pre-existing idea brought in from another experience. For whatever reason, they don't quite start from a blank page. They may bring in things from "previous" focal points in their existence, and sometimes people take on inharmonious genetic patterns or energetic beliefs. They do this knowingly of course.

If everything is happening at the same time, how can anyone "bring in" something from a past life?

Excellent question. The answer is simple: Part of their consciousness is still focused on another experience. They simply came here while still focusing on the energy of another situation, and that's neither good nor bad; it's simply a choice. Often times, a person will create an energetically similar situation in what is experienced as "this life" so that they can shift their consciousness and their perception and work things out in another arena – aka "this" existence.

Sort of like looking at a certain experience with a fresh set of eyes or with a different perspective.

Right. At some level the soul is wanting to further an experience, so one "lifetime" of stories carries over into "another." In truth, it's all the same. It's really all about perspective and choosing love.

What about being stuck? I've heard about people reliving certain patterns life in and life out.

Again, it's a choice. Many times, however, the person has forgotten they have a choice. They may have absorbed lifetimes of beliefs that back up their struggle. These beliefs of course are a direction of the energy, and until directed otherwise, the energy will continue to do what it was asked to do—in this case, keep the bad times coming.

How do we break that cycle then? How do we choose to become unstuck if we

> *a) don't know we have a choice, and*

> *b) don't even know we're stuck?*

By proclaiming to All That Is, "I Am Self-Love." In so doing, you invoke divine love—which *is* Self-Love—and you free yourself to choose. This causes a chain reaction in the whole of collective consciousness. Eventually, the entire vibration will rise beyond the tipping point, and as such this is a brief description of what you would call the ascension process.

What about genetic patterns and energetic beliefs? Why would I take on stuff like that? Why would I not be born just knowing my connection?

You've chosen to have a certain experience a certain way in a certain perceivable time/space moment. There is no other answer. Genetic beliefs – as all other beliefs – simply serve as contrast that allows for new areas of contrast which lead to new possibilities and greater expansion and awareness of self.

Everything is evolving, even what you consider to be God. God is the whole of creation and creation is constantly experiencing itself in new ways.

Wow. That's a concept.

Right? Sometimes, people choose to forget they have a choice. They hit a bit of a speed bump, forget who they really are, fear enters the equation, and they latch on to the closest thing that feels safe. In other words, they stop acting from the standpoint of self-creation start re-acting instead of acting. They give away their creation by believing in their smallness and lack of ability to create their desired outcome. Belief in lack and limitation forms for many reasons, but we would like to add that there is always an aspect of you—whether you consciously recognize it or not—that always knows its true connection and relation to Source. It is because of this knowing, that you are able to feel safe enough to enter this reality and "try the ride," in the first place. Some, however, forget all of this once the ride begins. This is neither good nor bad. Again, it's all choice, and it's all good.

Can we move on to thoughts as energy?

Sure, but it's not the long explanation you're looking for. Thoughts are simply energy. They are a form of communication both within and without. In other words, one of the ways you communicate with yourself is through thought. That should be obvious enough. Take an inventory right now. At any given moment, you may be having literally thousands of thoughts. You are consciously aware at any given moment of between three and ten depending on your capacity or mood. Thought then is also a means of communication with the universe; for thoughts are merely energy, and as such, they are always mingling and at play with the rest of creation. We say it is a means of communication within and without because, while everything is a manifestation of what is going on inwardly, your thoughts also permeate your energy field and extend beyond your body. This dichotomy becomes clear in the knowing that what is outside and what is inside are one and the same.

What just ran through my mind is the statement: "You are the God you've been praying to."

Yes. That is a perfect illustration of how all of this comes together. Many have chosen to experience the concept of God—and what we mean in this reference to God is the great creator being who created the earth—as something outside of their being (God experiencing God from the perspective of "separate" or "other"). They do not consciously choose to know that they are god. The parallel concept here is that like the universe, god is that which you are. Your understanding of god has been created from fear and separation, and it has thereby been placed into what you would term the ethos or culture—the out there. It is a force outside of you. In the same regard, you have placed the universe outside of yourself. You are made of the same "stuff." I am not talking of the gas that makes up one star or the matter that makes up a planet.

Whoa. Wait a minute. You just said, "I." Who are you?

I am the Godhead. I am that which you also are, and you are that which I am.

So, are you like my higher self?

In a way, but I am a more unified and encompassing understanding of that concept. I am the consciousness of all that you have been, and all that will come to be. I am the totality of the "you" who has been individualized. You could say I am the You behind the "you."

How are you different from pure Source or All That Is?

I am pure Source, and I am an individualized aspect. I wanted to simply show you that individualization continues in ways you do not understand- even when you are wrapped up in the totality of Pure Source. You never become lost or dissipated. You become pure positive energy. You become pure, positive love, but individuality persists because to Source, separation never existed. In actuality, there is no difference between the "we" and the "I." What better way to illustrate what we have been talking about with regard to separating from Source. You have moved to the point of accepting that "we" are one, but as soon as an "I" enters the equation, you separate. Do you understand?

I think so, but if there is no separation, how can there be individuality?

Remember, you are an individualized aspect – a pixel within a picture of a picture. You, however, have within yourself the ability to unify your knowing and project forth into this reality as a single entity – the totality of that picture. This is brought forth now, so that you may see the relevance between that which you call god, and thought—or that which you are.

I was just about to ask if you were saying: I am thought, and I just went to "I think, therefore I am."

Yes.

So then, do I not think when I die?

Yes. And you shall still be, as you always are. But, you are not getting the correlation. Just as god is a thought to you, so too are you a thought to yourself. This was the nature of your birth. You were literally thought into being.

By myself?

By yourself as Source Energy.

Wow. I thought this was going to be a more "thoughts create your reality" kind of chapter.

Think deeper. If thoughts create reality, what created you?

When you say it that way, I start to get it. So, thoughts basically form the web of my existence?

Yes. We like that imagery. You not only use your thoughts via your internal mind speak, but through them, you send out waves and pictures and vibrations and thus shape your entire world. We would now like to give you a wonderful exercise with which to plug into the flow of all that you are with regard to your individual creation. We have discussed energy with you, but we wish to show you just how much of your creation is yours. You see, you grasp the concept of thoughts creating reality, but when it comes down to your individual responsibility for creation, you sometimes think, "Well, that's just the way the cookie crumbles." We would like to show you that you are the cookie.

Ready?

Okay.

You asked earlier about knowing if you're stuck. If you feel stuck, you most likely will be. Whether you were stuck because you were actually stuck, or because you became focused on being stuck does not matter. We simply want to show you how easy it can be to become unstuck.

We're going to ask you to play with us, and that you play along with yourself. If you feel resistance, if you feel that you have hit a lid or a glass ceiling, or even a giant wall, this is okay. In fact, it is good. It will help us show you how to erase the boundaries and remove boulders you have placed before you.

Go within. Find your I Am presence.

My I Am who?

Find the part of you that knows it is Source Energy.

Gotcha.

Feel yourself with relation to this part of you? Are you old friends, or are you meeting consciously for the first time? Realize that this part of you, and the part that thinks you are separate are the same. They are both you. If you have any fear coming to the surface, move into love. Claim, "I Am Self-Love." Love yourself enough to continue. You are only playing with energy. You are not committing to anything at this moment; you can always go back. Right now, just be.

Feel yourself blend with this wonderful part of you that is Source Energy. See yourself as a fluid, light-like substance. The two of you become one moving field of love. Now, where would you like to go? What would you like to experience? Whatever you want to see come into your life, flow into that thing. Bring your energy into that space. Take an inventory of how you feel. Begin to fill this space with all the things you want. Flow into the energy of having everything you desire. If you hit a wall, pause. Allow the wall to drop through the floor. It's been placed there by you, and you have all right and authority to simply let it fall down.

May we use you to show the reader what we're talking about?

Sure. I'll play along.

What would you like to experience?

How about being rich?

You mean you'd like to have a lot of money?

Yes.

That's probably quite a common desire.

Start by becoming one with your Presence—
All that you are. Allow yourself to flow into what
having money looks like.

Will you explain your process for the benefit of
the reader?

*Well, I flowed up a hill into a really nice house. I
went past my cars and into my giant home, and
then it got lonely. I couldn't really bring in
anything else because I got stuck in that feeling.*

This is not the first place you have fallen out
with regard to money, but it is one that is
obvious. You are holding the belief that you do
not deserve to have all of these things without
someone to share them with. Ergo, you are not
enough.

Wow.

Wow, indeed. Let that go. Bring in some dogs.
(Pause) That did the trick. That opened your
heart. We don't want you focusing on a situation
in which there is absolutely anything that will
cause you to recoil or stop.

Now, can you be in the experience of what
having money is like without bringing in all the
other things you associate with it?

This is interesting to me, but no. I keep going to "there's no one else here."

So you see you are also holding that money equals being alone. It should be noted that when we first tried this exercise, your first thought was to start with relationships, but you changed your mind and went to money. You thought you could avoid looking at your junk. Sorry, buddy. It's time to bring all the junk up so you can let it out.

Okay, so what are we doing?

We're showing you that you are creating from such a limiting perspective. You are bringing in every story you've ever told yourself about creating money. You think you want money, but you have 9,412 beliefs that you're lugging around with you that are saying something contrary. This is just one example. Flow into what having money looks like one more time. Go back to your house, past your new cars, and into your house. See your dogs.

Now when these relationship ideas pop up, simply allow them to drop out. If you must have a relationship, shift your focus and be in a relationship with yourself. (Pause) It sounded silly, but it moved your energy, did it not?

Yes. It did.

Whenever you wish to create something, go out and feel its creation. You've wanted an iPad for several weeks now, but you refused to buy what you wanted because you were in a "lack" consciousness. We asked you to visualize buying an iPad, and the first thing you energetically went to was the experience of not being able to afford one. You may not have even known you were this stuck with regard to money. In this instance, every time you thought about doing what you wanted, you sent the universe a message that said "More poor, please." By letting that go and just flowing out into the energy and experiencing buying it, you freed up a lot of energy. It will now be much easier to attract the money it will take to buy the iPad.

You could feel the walls you put up, could you not?

Yes, I could.

Energetically experience the things you would like to bring into your life. If you find there are stumbling blocks, allow the blocks to fall away. They are your blocks, and you no longer need them. These things that block you from energetically flowing into this scenario are the same blocks that will keep you from manifesting what you want in the physical world. Don't get into your head and try to move them from there, because your head did not put them there. Your energy did. Your feelings did. Your fears did. Allow yourself to say: "These fears don't need to be here right now because I am only playing." Send them away and continue building your life.

What does that have to do with being stuck?

You have asked how to know if you are stuck. If you cannot energetically experience the things you want, and you know that the energy is what creates everything, how will you create them? You will not. You will become stuck. This is simply a way to un-stick yourself early in the process. As you are letting go, you are moving energy. It is much easier to move energy when it is in this state. In knowing that you are only playing, you can allow your fear to subside. You can then see what it would be like to have what you want. Having it in a fear-free environment helps to release the fear in the physical plane. It helps you move energy that needs to be moved, and it helps you release the stories you no longer need.

As you flow into new creations, notice when you leave the state of pure love. When you leave this state, you have encountered something within your story that you may wish to release. It is always up to you. Know that when you take this journey, you are not being asked to physically have any experience other than what you are creating right now. You are simply asking yourself to feel the possibilities of an infinite field. To create your situation from fear or restraint is lack. To choose from possibilities among possibilities is true abundance. For then, all things are possible.

Chapter Three

Divine-Right Destiny and Self-Creation

Most people living within this plane of existence perceive that they have a "destiny." We would like to explain what this feeling represents.

Okay.

It can be many things: the remembrance of a desire from before physical incarnation was chosen. It can be your desire to form or to move in a certain direction. But its implication is incorrect because there is no thing which you must do in this life. There is no thing you were specifically put here to do. You chose to come here with your desires. You chose to come here with your creative abilities, and this sense of greater purpose, of destiny, is a wonderful remembrance of all your possibilities.

So this is not like "soul" school?

Right. Source isn't grading or judging you. It's simply smiling—coming forth within you— whispering: "Remember." Remember what you wanted to do. Remember who you are. Remember your dreams; follow them. It's good to follow your dreams. It's good to create what you want. It's good that you remember who you are.

I thought good and bad were just judgments?

Were not saying "good" in the sense that it's bad to do the opposite. We're using the term "good" because following your hearts truest desires <u>feels</u> good, and when you <u>feel</u> good, you're in a state of allowance, and when you are in allowance, you are in love. When you're in love, you pave the way for the expansion of consciousness. You pave the way for All That Is.

Whatever you want, whatever you wish to accomplish, is your divine right, and therefore its accomplishment is your divine-right destiny. Know that *whatever* you do is your destiny, for there is no right, there is no wrong.

This doesn't mean you don't have a purpose. In fact, your purpose is what it's always been: to create. Your purpose is to love yourself. Your purpose is to have the full experience of that which you are.

So how then, does this relate to Self-Love?

We wanted to show you that the idea that you have of "destiny" is also a story. You have not only stories of what has shaped you and what you have become, and why you have become that, but you also have stories of what you want to become. You have stories of what you believe you must become, and these are just stories. These are also ideas you must let go of—not that you can't follow your dreams; we want you to follow your dreams, but let go of <u>why</u> you think these are your dreams. Let go of any sort of conditions, any sort of pressures, any sort of right and wrong, or "musts." Pursue your dreams because they are your desires, not because you <u>must</u> pursue them. remember, life isn't a race. Fulfillment is not a challenge. As with expansion, there is no final destination, no "there" to get to. So listen to your heart. Allow your creation and your self the freedom to grow, expand, and change. When you accomplish one thing, you will wish to accomplish more. Therefore, it is your desire that you should follow—not preexisting ideas of why you should do something.

And Self-Love?

When you can truly love your self and release all of your stories, you're free to move about in your creation, and you also free your creation to grow. You free your creation just as you yourself have been freed by Source: You were created, and you were given free will, and you were given room to grow. And when we say "created," we mean *you* were that which created you, but you did not hold you back. You didn't program yourself. You suggested areas of exploration. You outlined certain possibilities, but you gave yourself the freedom to come in and experience and to change, to desire and to create new things, and to create new desires and to allow those changes and desires to unfold. Therefore, when you can claim Self-Love, when you can *be* Self-Love, when you can know that there is no separation, when you can truly love yourself and focus on that love, you can go wherever you wish to go, and you go there in freedom. The creation is freedom, and the creation is freed.

That's pretty open-ended.

Absolutely, it is.

When this happens, you'll find that where you thought you were going will become that much greater than what you thought it would be, because you've released it and given it room to grow. So release the idea or story of destiny as a set-in-stone future so that you can become free to truly choose in every moment who you are and who you will become.

Well how do I know this will work? How do I know when it is working?

To be in Self-Love is to know that it is working. To love yourself is to know yourself is to be yourself is to create yourself.

I don't think that's really what I asked.

It is; we'll explain. At first, trust. Move into trust. If you can't trust yourself, you can't trust the divine. If you can't trust the divine, you can't trust yourself. Around all of this, claim: "I am Self-Love." In the last chapter, we gave you an exercise as well as some suggestions to show you how you may vibrationally and energetically tap into your energy and see how that works, but we believe what you have asked just now is "how can you know?"

Right.

Okay. Many people say "I must create in order to know that I am the creator," and we say, "You must know that you are the creator in order to create." Why? When you are aware and focused on Self-Love, you will totally feel it. You will know it. You will be Self-Love. Therefore, you will know Self-Love. We know this is a difficult explanation, so we will put it another way: choose to know it works.

That seems like a cop-out.

But it's not; it's your choice that's always at play. When you can choose to know something, when you choose to choose that something, you are directing your energy. This is what you must do: You must choose. You must choose to know. You must choose to love yourself. You must choose to choose love. When you can do this there will be no doubt, for your world, your creation, your own self, will show up differently. You will feel it.

So take us back to creation, and how all of this relates to what and how I create.

Sure. You came forth through a strong desire to experience yourself. The self that you are now experiencing is the result of that desire. Within that desire, were thoughts of how the experience would be. Thus, you began not as a twinkle in your father's eye, but as a twinkle in your own.

We've come here through our desire for an experience of oneness with you – which was triggered by your desire to experience oneness with us. Oneness (this experience) is your vibrational match. Therefore, all that we are—which is all that you are—is able to come together in this way because *you* have asked, because *we* have asked. There is nothing that cannot be accomplished through allowing. We have said to you that your thoughts create your reality, and we wish to show you the extent to which this is true. For you do not come into this reality as what you would call the blank page. You come into this reality because you have a thought; you had the desire for the creation of an experience. As consciousness on this plane has moved, there's been an asking by many that creation become a little easier.

It's a fast food Universe.

The point is, it has always been fast, but it's a process created by you. As you expand, you form a new desire, and through that desire comes thought, and in a limitless, resistance-free environment, that thought immediately becomes reality. What has happened on this plane is that you have allowed a belief in separation to form a delay in your creation. You then focus on the delay, which creates more delay. We know this sounds remedial, but it is the truth.

So how do thoughts create your reality?

You know that scientifically, what you focus on appears. There is a wonderful theory that was once rather revolutionary but is now rather basic.

It states that when an electron is observed, it acts like a particle. When that energy is not observed, it takes on the properties of a wave. Therefore, the focus has literally changed the energy. Now here is a keeper: Thought is also vibration—just like a molecule, an electron, and even space. Remember, there is always a thinker behind the thought.

Wait. So, if focus changes the energy, how does that affect thought? By changing thought, don't you change the vibration?

Indeed you do. Not only do your thoughts create based on their vibration, but they are also vibrations in and of themselves. Think of it in terms of an economic belief. If you believe that you have to work hard in order to make money, your world will show up accordingly. You can think happy thoughts all day, but if the underlying energy is "I have to work hard to make money," you will always have to work hard to make money. By balancing the vibrations around why you think you have to work hard to make money, you can let that story go and form a new thought – which then replaces the old belief system.

So literally, everything is vibration?

Precisely. If you look at the world as one giant vibratory being—and it is a being very much alive—you realize that there are all kinds of levels within this being . . . even see your self as a vibrational being, as a vibration within a larger vibration. Your thoughts are then a vibration within the larger vibration that is you. Your desires, your wants, your beliefs, all of these are vibrations. When you issue forth thought, it appears to you as an idea, as a wanting, as a concept, but as you offer up this thought, you are offering up energy. Thought is merely the picture that accompanies the vibration, and when we say to you "give up your story and be the blank page," we're saying detach the mental images, the pictures that accompany the vibration of you, because when you can do that, you free the vibration to manifest in ways your conscious mind might never have imagined or allowed.

So the best way to get what I want is to totally let go of it?

You don't let go of the vibration. You let go of the attachment as well as how you think it should look—from the delivery to manifestation and beyond. You see, when you send out thought, a vibration is released into the field of larger vibration, and it seeks out its match. Often times, when you send out a vibration with an image, picture, or idea attached, those images and pictures and ideas limit the vibration. So you say, "I have asked for this, but I have received this other thing," and we say to you that the other thing you have received is that which you have asked for. So, what you must do, is release.

And, again, how do thoughts create?

The vibration is sent out from you like that of a musical note. It goes out and resonates into the field of energy that you are, and your universe is created accordingly. Remember, you've created it so that it will answer every vibrational "phone call" you place.

So it's more a bottoms-up, rather than a top-down concept?

Yes, in a manner of speaking. Thoughts are *literally* the *vibrations* you *live in,* and you have the creative authority to change those thoughts which will in turn change your world. You think of the world as a large mass vibration of energy, and you think you are a smaller vibration living within it when in actuality, the smaller vibrations - smaller in your eyes - are the vibrations that create and sustain the larger. This is creation. What you focus on <u>does</u> in fact appear. You have appeared here because you—as source energy—have focused on you, and as this purest form of source energy focused upon YOU, YOU sprang forth. So, there is not this giant, judgmental creator entity in the sky looking down. Rather, it's You - You at your pure source level, focusing on and loving you. The extent to which you can allow this love to physically permeate your reality is the extent to which you can love your self, allow thoughts to align, and to create your world and experience.

The vibration is sent forth from YOUR thought—and we would mention that the thought you're sending out does not always match the vibration you are in. You can have a thought or wish to have more money while your vibration is "I don't have any money." Therefore, what comes back to you through the Law of attraction is the lack of money, more bills, more debt, and insufficient funds. You that you have the energy, the access, and the knowledge to change that. There is not anything outside of your self that you have to do or be to have everything that you want. The key to everything is Self-Love, because when you can love your self—and we're talking about real divine cosmic love, no judgment—you love everything because you are all there is.

Every thought you offer is offered in the vibration of love, abundance, and of peace and joy, and your universe unfolds accordingly. Now when you ask for something—no matter the size or cost—and your vibration matches the thought, the universe—meaning you—will begin taking steps to fulfill your desire.

That's a little more complicated than I imagined.

You want simple? When the sustained expansion of the vibration is joyous and matched by your thoughts, what will happen as the universe unfolds is that you will meet up with another desire and another and a chain reaction will occur. Sometimes you ask and you immediately receive; other times, you ask and receive a little, but another door has opened, and you walk through that door and you receive a little more. Then you walk through another door, and you receive even more, and as you continue to receive and want more, new realities are forming which in turn form new desires. But if you offer forth the thought that "I would like this," but your vibration does not match, you won't get what you think you're asking for. You get what you are vibrationally resonating with. The key is to stay in love.

Yes, that's always been my challenge: how do I stay in love?

Just continue to claim "I Am Self-Love."

All right; I Am Self-Love.

You are now in love, and it's that easy if you continue to choose it.

What you're saying is my thoughts create my reality because my reality is basically a large system of vibrations?

Yes, that is quite good.

So, my reality is a large system of vibrations that is created or sustained by the vibrations that are me?

Yep. You got it.

So when you say "thought creates reality," a more accurate statement would be "vibration creates reality."

Vibration is reality. Thoughts create.

Interesting. So the thought is the asking and also the receiving?

The thought is the asking. The vibration is the desire to form the new creation. The thought is the creation. So, within a system of vibration,

vibration is the language. Vibration is the water which gives life. Vibration is everything. Thought directs the vibration. Thought is the coming together of the vibrations and the desires and wants which then create your reality.

So everything really is related?

Down the rabbit hole we go.

Chapter Four

Self-Love/New Thought

We've told you that Self-Love is the most important factor in creation, and we want to explain why. You see, all separation - whether it is you from your self, you from the God you are, you from your creation, or you from your desire - is simply the dis-allowance of Self-Love.

The glue that connects everything.

Precisely. In the allowance of love, you are in the allowance of flow. All that is and the potential for all that will be streams forth from your consciousness. Divine love is the love for which, the love in which, you—your creation, your expression—knows no bounds. To experience divine love directed at the source—divine love *of who you are from all you are and vice versa*—is to truly free up your vibrations and free your being. It is to release your resistance and to truly move into creation. We've said that resistance and struggle are a manifestation of a dis-allowance of Self-Love, and we wish to make it clear to you that _all_ struggle and _all_ wanting that goes unfulfilled is a direct result of the non-allowance of Self-Love. The creation that you see manifest is

69

directly proportional to the amount of divine love you have for your self. *Therefore, it is really Self-Love.*

Vibrationally you call forth that which you are asking. In the same way, you _allow_ that which you are asking, allowing yourself to both ask and to receive, through divine love. This becomes an important distinction because, if you ask in a vibration of knowing and receiving, and you send forth the vibration of what you are asking for— the universe will always answer that call by sending you what you've asked for.

You said earlier that asking was different than allowing.

If it's not in the same vibration, that's true. We were referring to the vibration in which you ask. Most times, when you ask for something—you say wistfully, "I would like this thing." What you are really doing is being wishy-washy. It's like asking for a new car, while kicking the old car in the tire. You must ask with the knowledge that you are worthy, ask out of Self-Love, and then you will receive whatever you ask for. Period. It is not a question of whether you deserve it, or whether you have to do something physically to get it, and unless you add those things, you won't. You have to love yourself, demand what you want, and release it all.

Well, this brings up another question. You keep talking about love, and it seems to me that there are quite a lot of ass-holes in the world who get exactly what they want - sometimes at the expense of others - who don't seem to have a lot of love.

Interesting. Your consciousness did not initially plan to discuss this concern at this juncture, but that is the beauty of creation. When you trust and let go, your plans go out the window, and the universe takes over. For the benefit of the reader, we would like to mention that this channel came via dictation, and that now, in the reading and experiencing of this information, a new question, a new desire, has arisen.

Seems like every question/answer expands the playing field.

Indeed. First of all, we would like to tell you that which you already know: You are in judgment of those whom you perceive as getting what they want at the expense of others. We also wish to tell you that despite appearances, nothing is ever at the expense of another. If someone appears to be taken advantage of, it is because

71

there is something within their energy that either believes it needs this experience, or a variation there of. Situations are always a vibrational match to all parties who are experiencing them. Judging people as not having much love for others or themselves is based on your idea of love - the story of love - that you have. They love themselves in that they have no judgment about what they want. They simply want it, and they seek out ways of getting it however they can. They love themselves enough to allow what they want as far as satisfying their desires.

That seems rather cold-hearted. (Pause) Yes, I know: another judgment.

Indeed, and it may seem that way. But again, those people will only attract into their lives and business dealings those who share their belief structures—whether that be someone who feels they must be taken advantage of, or someone who believes they must always be less than, etc. You see from this example that you are still holding a story of what love looks like. Often times, people have drawn a line in the sand between the consciousness of what they see as love, the Christ consciousness—love of all, oneness—and the consciousness of "I want what I want and I'm going to get it." They don't' view the latter as love, only as self-aggrandizement, yet the universe doesn't judge. It doesn't say: "Well, he has no judgment or belief preventing the manifestation of what he is asking for, but he's a jack-ass so we're gonna make him sweat and go without. Vibrationally, no resistance is a form of love.

But not divine love?

No, but not in the sense you mean: lower/higher. However, when you can marry the two: love, or no resistance, and oneness or love of all that is, your experience will be divine. The speed and directness with which you receive what you are asking for, and how closely the manifestation resembles what you <u>think</u> you've truly asked for, is all directly related to the amount of allowance you hold—that is, the divine love you have, the love of your self, the love of all that you are, the love of your desire, the love of creation, and your ability to receive through that love. Love is the gate through which all things must enter. Release your picture of love so that you may experience it in all its wondrous manifestations.

Wow. I need a minute to digest that. I guess it makes sense. I mean, if we are all the creators of our reality, then . . . So there aren't any universal brownie points for being good?

Or merit badges. Good is a judgment. Now, certain vibrations <u>feel</u> better, and certain vibrations bring more of that which you call love into the picture, and since love is the glue that holds things together, as you said earlier, more harmony results. But good and bad are judgments. On the level of receiving, the universe doesn't judge. Vibrationally, no resistance is a form of love, but when you can marry that love with the love of all, or when you can move from just loving the individualized you into the expansion of the you who is the all, everything will come in greater ways than you can imagine.

In other words, it goes beyond just loving yourself and getting what you want.

Yes, and at the same time, there is no goal to reach. You are here to feel good, and divine love feels good. In a place of total divine love, there is no judgment—that which you call good or bad. There simply is no judgment, and in a place where there is no judgment, that which is called forth, simply comes. So in a way, you could look at it, in your lingo—that divine love is not only the allowing, but it is like a booster pack, a rocket pack, strapped to your desire, that both hurries the placement of the order as well as hastens its delivery—the manifestation. Sleep on it. We have a feeling we'll be coming back to this.

Okay, but in the mean time, can you explain how this relates to the idea of thinking a new thought?

Ah. Perfect! We've spoken to you about new thought, and in order to understand new thought, we have to go back and say once again that you must lose all old thought—old thoughts being the way in which you think about yourself, about your world, the way in which you define your self, or make up who you are. By this we mean not just the job you hold or the appearance you have - your weight or your height - but also the emotional stories you carry around: the memories, the childhoods, the experiences, the associations with the past, even what you call love and the judgments that carries. All of these factors - whether you are consciously aware of them or not - create your reality. You are defining your self by descriptions that are no longer valid. Definitions are sort of like locked in beliefs which continue to replicate themselves ad infinitum until they are changed.

Like the software program in The Matrix?

That's one way of understanding it, yes. You've chosen to experience these things, and you've been told you must place value upon what you've experienced. In placing value upon it, you empower it and it helps define that which you are creating. You make it a part of who you are, and it is not a part of who you are. It is only a part of that which you have called forth to experience so that you can have new desires, yet you hold on to the "facts." You hold on to the experience, and it limits that which you are. It limits that which you can call forth because everything has been shaded and colored by what has already been. We are here to tell you: that which you are is source energy. Anything else on top of that is your story—something that you have learned, or has been added to you—and getting back to that pure state, that pure knowing, that pure un-attachment to everything, is where the magic is because there is no attachment. There is no definition. There is no expectation. There is only love.

And this is where Self-Love comes in?

Yes, because it is the perfect environment for *all that you are* to experience itself and to form new desires: one of which is the desire to think a new thought. Now, we know what you are thinking: "How can there be a new thought?" Most of the thoughts that have been thought in your consciousness are on repeat mode. They are on a loop. In the past hundred years, there has been an outpouring of new inventions and inspired ideas. Well, those inspired ideas are new thoughts. How often do you think new thoughts? If you are still clinging to the story of who you are, you are unable to think a new thought about your self because there is no room. Your space for definitions has already been filled.

And the same applies to images, right? Like, how I think things should look?

Of course. With creation, you offer forth vibrations, as we have said, and often times you have a picture in your mind of how the manifestation should look, what the process should be like, and we are saying to you that this is a picture - or a series of pictures - that actually hinders the universe from bringing in what you've asked it to bring.

Well, that brings up the question of visualization. Does this mean that visualizing what you want is not a good idea? I realize that visualizing something does limit it, but doesn't it also help define what it is you're asking for?

We would answer that by simply exploring the subject in a broader sense. Visualizations are great because of the vibrations they bring about, but often the person gets so caught up in the physical things they may want, that they begin to focus on a vibration that might not be the quickest route.

What do you mean?

If you want a new car, and you visualize it, but somewhere in your past, you have formed a negative or limiting belief about purchasing a new car (I don't deserve one, they cost too much, the economy is too bad, or anything else your mind—whether subconscious or not—associates with getting or having a new car) by visualizing that car, you might also be unknowingly activating an old or limiting belief.

When you are in a total state of limitlessness and allowance—total Self-Love—everything just is. Everything can roll on in because you have gotten out of your own way. So, it's not that visualizations are in themselves "good or bad," it's just that coming from Self-Love can bypass all of the little human tricks you sometimes use to keep yourselves from actually getting what you want.

We would also like to add that if someone experienced more of a high from the visualization than they did from the actual manifestation, the peptides in their body would seek out that high over and over.

Because they prefer the rush?

Yes. On a chemical level, your body (which is a physical expression of your energy) is telling the universe "hold off, because if I get that, it won't feel as good as the rush I get from wanting." Therefore you'd wind up in a state where you would be "doing everything right," but wherein nothing was materializing.

I think I've actually caught myself saying those exact words.

So you see, letting go of the story is not just letting go of who you think you are, not just letting go of your identity, it is literally letting go of expectation, of attachment, of every definition, and when you can do that, you can truly move into expansion. And that will bring in another new thought, which will create another new desire, which will create another new experience, and so on and so forth. This is how expansion occurs.

This is—for lack of a better term—the story of expansion, which even we are asking ourselves to release so that expansion can come in new and unexpected ways. You see, all energy is trying to make something from a certain recipe, and we are saying that you cannot make brownies using the recipe for a chocolate chip cookie, and in essence that is what we are all doing by holding onto our stories. We are saying "this is what I would like to make," but the ingredients we are using don't add up.

And the recipe for the new human?

It's been a while since mankind has had a new thought with regard to who you are. Thousands of years ago, Christ brought forth the thought that "I am one with God;" Buddha brought forth the thought, "I am one with the all." Throughout time, every now and then a new thought has emerged, but on a mass scale it's not happened for thousands of years. However, the asking for greater expansion has grown, and it is now time not just for one new thought, but for <u>all</u> new thought. Your physical world is changing because your vibrational consciousness is changing. New thoughts are forming in the collective consciousness, in the individuals. New thoughts of your possibilities are forming everywhere, every day, and because of this expansion your world is now in the midst - in the very beginnings - of what will be a dramatic change.

For thousands of years this change has been discussed, talked about, prophesied, and only recently has the thought formed that this change could happen as the result of an awakening of consciousness. The thought has come forth that it does not have to come about through wars or suffering or the ascent of a physical savior, for the true savior is the risen consciousness. This is new thought. The quantum physics of spirituality have emerged. This is new thought. There is a science of no separation emerging. This is new thought. When the vibrations are clean, the new thoughts can grow. What we mean by clean is that they are balanced. Their polarities, their dualities, their opposites are all balanced within the one.

Again, that happens how?

As you allow Self-Love, the vibrations become clean, they become balanced. Clean is not to say that they were dirty in a negative way, but we mean clean as in they become bright, they become crystal clear, they become sure about that which they are, and in that knowing, is sparked a new thought. In those new thoughts are the vibrations of the current universe unfolding. Thus is the ascension process you hear so much about these days.

Chapter Five

Expansion

There is a common conception about consciousness that we wish to address. To call it a misconception would be false; however, we wish to correct the notion that ascension is a movement of upward motion or energy. We wish to correct the belief that consciousness is moving from low to high. The idea of the ascension as a ladder is not correct, a holdover perhaps from *Jacob's Ladder* in the Bible. A more accurate way to explain the process would be to call it an expansion.

I've always thought of ascension as transcending this plane.

Well, prepare to let go of that story and have a new thought.

Okay. Expand my mind.

We hope to expand more, but the mind is a start. We'd like to move out of "ascension" and into "expansion" with regard to the language of consciousness. For a very long time, many have held to a particular story of ascension, and we think it would be easier to let go of that definition by replacing the term. With regard to their conception, ascension has been considered a journey to God – God here being a destination, whether physical or spiritual. In truth, that which you call God, you already are. By letting go of definitions—again, becoming the blank page—you can allow *all that you are* to be remembered. Such definitions and stories have been holding closed the doorway to these memories, and in letting them go, you are inviting the knowledge of *all that you are* to come forth and make itself known to the conscious mind, be it an individual or the collective.

In other words, I'm not trying to get anywhere with regard to a spiritual or even a physical "heaven?"

Precisely. You are already here—we say here because you can never be there—with there being away, or in another place from that which you presently occupy. You are here now, you have just forgotten.

That sounds like one of those hokey new age sayings: "remember what you've forgotten."

That doesn't make it incorrect. You yourself have read the Bible. Did Jesus not say that what you call the kingdom is within? This teaching was correct. The Gnostic gospels went a step further in quoting Jesus as saying that you could split open a piece of wood and therein also find the kingdom. This is the equivalent of what we have said: everything is energy. That which you have called God is energy and is the source of everything. It is everything. Yes, you can journey to other dimensions upon your perceived death in this reality, and you can reincarnate whenever and wherever you may choose, but wherever you go, "there you are," as they say. And what you are, is God. So there is no heavenly destination. There is no "there" to get to. That is a story which has perpetuated a stalled consciousness. We are asking to release that and experience the glory of that which we are—that which you are.

"A stalled consciousness?" Isn't that a contradiction? I thought that with everything being energy, we were constantly expanding like the universe itself.

Yes. However, your understanding of expansion is not clear as of yet. We will address expansion, but first let us explain what we mean by a "stalled consciousness."

Obviously, consciousness is expanding. That much is true. However, as we have said, the thoughts of who you are—your ability to own your creatorship and feel good about it—have been seemingly stuck in denial. You've been in denial of your Godhood. As you refused to know that you are God, you placed your creatorship outside of yourselves and placed it in the hands of another. Some placed it in the hands of religion, while others denied the very existence of any such force at all. Others gave their creatorship away to the belief that they were living as a consequence of deeds done in "other" lives, be it past or future. All of these are ways in which you have denied your self. In this state of self-denial, consciousness experienced all of the wonderful creations and experiences that come about as the result from such beliefs. These experiences have been wonderful, a great learning for you to have created them. They are the experiences that have called forth the expansion into knowing. We could add that experiencing your own godhood was a thought that was unavailable to most of the collective consciousness until recently.

So we're on the move?

Oh, yes. You're always moving. Even in giving over your creatorship, you're still creating. You're creating the experience of living a disempowered existence wherein you simply don't know you are

God. As we've said, in the notion that God or Nirvana or Heaven - or whatever you wish to call it - is someplace else, there is the belief that you must then "get there" in order to have the experience of oneness. It creates a vertical view of expansion. "I am a lower being trying to reach a higher state." In actuality, there is no higher state. No state of awareness is "higher" than another. At the level of oneness, you have simply shed all of your stories. Again, remember the metaphor of the hologram, each piece separate and whole at the same time.

Many people define expansion by what they have accomplished - their spiritual merit badges. The real expansion is in letting go of all of it— letting go of who you think you are and how you have defined yourself and your relationship to everyone and every thing, including all beliefs. We're not saying quit your job and go into a vegetative state. We're just saying that when you can let it all go, you are living in the creation of the moment. You're not tied to thoughts of the future, or the past. Your creation is not tied down by anything. You are able to be in that pure moment from which all creation comes. In this state, you're creating exactly as you direct. You are still you, you are just a "you" that is much bigger and the direction more expansive.

So expansion is not an up/down, or even a side-to-side experience. It is sort of without borders or boundaries?

Yes. It is just what it is called: expansion. It is not circular; it is not a spiraling of consciousness; it is not a ladder that you must spiritually climb, and while it is none of those things, it is all of those things at the same time.

I think I understand that, but can you put it a little more simply?

Yes, we can. It has no limits and is undefined. It is all, and it is ever experiencing itself in ways that create new desires that create new experiences—thus, expansion.

Hmmm... Cool.

Yep. Do you have something else for us to clarify?

Well, I'd like to talk a little more about ascension, or expansion as you've defined it, and how our story and relationship to that concept is changing.

Well, we've spoken to you of your thoughts and your vibration, and we have mentioned polarities. I believe that we . . .

You just said I.

Indeed. You are focusing on me – you are focusing on you, and within the "we," is the "I." The "we" is the "I." That might make a good chapter title. Remember that.

I'd like to address it now, if you don't mind.

Of course we don't mind, not that we have one in the singular sense to mind. "We" refers to both the collection of our energy, and the physically focused portion of "your" energy. In reality - if we may use that word - we are all one energy.

I get that, but...

To a point. You can understand and accept that there is a part of you that is broader than the "you" that is physically on the planet, and you think of that part of you just as you think of yourself in physical existence. We come to you as just another aspect of that which you are. You have just realized that you think of us as you, yet you do not call us by your name. You then see that part of you as a part of another collection of energy—and within that energy you see separation via colors and light. You also see that group as a part of the energy of those whom you know as Christ and St. Germaine, etc. In truth, all of these energies work together because as you chase down the roots, you see that they are not roots. They are in fact one root.

Wow. So, it's really all just layers of the same thing?

Indeed, and even those layers are just illusions. You have done well in releasing the illusion of separation, yet we do not think that up until now you have realized just how "one" we are. It's a very big whole. We say we because to your mind—and currently to your energy, although this is changing—you see all of us as distinct energies. At different points of this process, you have focused on certain aspects of the energy—thus the usage of "I" where you expected a "we." You simply asked a question of the one consciousness, and allowed yourself to receive an answer from within one of the "layers." Remember, everything is happening at once, and . . .

Whoa. Stop right there. Let's go back to the clock example from chapter One. How can everything be happening at once, while we are expanding and experiencing new thought? That doesn't make sense to me.

It may be difficult to understand from the perspective of your "there," but all energy exists right now—in this moment. Everything that exists—dimensionally, in time—all of it, exists in potentialities. Remember the particle/wave experiment from quantum physics. The shared experience of the one is quite grand. Remember, you are focused in a particular time/space point of creation. We are beyond that point, yet we are also experiencing the potentiality of our "layer." Remember that everything is a vibration within a vibration within a vibration. So, in saying that— expand your perception of dimensions, of time, of all, and know that your clock example could be seen as a clock within a clock within a clock.

Like the Mandelbrot Set!?

Yes. It goes on forever. Our experience of it is expanding as our consciousness expands. And again, beneath it all, we are already where we are going.

This is why we wish to move from thoughts of vertical ascension and into expansion without boundaries. Where we are is perfect. We are choosing to have the experience. Therefore, do not wish to escape from this plane, for there is no place in which to escape to. If you feel the need to escape, shift your focus from escape to expansion—because focusing on escape will create the very perception you are trying to remove yourself from. You can never remove yourself from a perception because you are the one perceiving, and all you are experiencing is your perception. Remember this: you are here because here is fun. Here is YOU!

Chapter Six

The Unfolding - We are One

The universe did not start, as some theorize, in a giant big bang. Rather, it started with the big desire. It started with the desire by source to experience itself in a new way. There was a desire to experience the self. Your universe formed and took shape as a place of great potential through the one's desire to experience itself in an individualized form. As gases collided and particles expanded, there was a great unfolding that took place; and in this unfolding, there was the continual desire for experience, for growth, and for expansion. Thus is the story of creation, the template for all that is, including the human race.

But I thought we were losing our stories.

Ah. Very good. We have told you that with your stories come limitations. So we ask you, what is the limitation of this story?

It's the belief that I have to choose one potential over another, right?

In a way. At this time, you do not believe that it is possible to experience multidimensionality in the physical form, yet physical is just an aspect of spiritual. You exist everywhere at all times. You are very aware that you travel to "other" realms during sleep, yet these "other" realms are just as much a part of your existence as your physically focused being. You have simply limited your physical choices through your perception and thus limited the creation of your physical environment. What we wish to ask of you is that you begin to release the either/or, here/there, physical/nonphysical choice aspect of your creation story. For in doing so, you may come to remember that in order to be god, you do not have to treat yourself as only a part of god. That is to say, you may be it all.

Okay. And since you've brought up the beginnings of the universe, can we talk about how that unfolding occurred?

Certainly.

Well, you said that gases collided and particles expanded, but what was here before that?

You are asking how the material elements took shape and where they originated.

Yes.

They came from you. Within your body is infinite space. At the quantum level, none of the particles touch. Solid matter is just an illusion. You've read about that, right?

Yes. I'm familiar with that theory.

It is more than theory. It is true. And indeed beyond atoms, you will find pure vibration – which brings us to the concept of imaging frequency. The technology will come, and you will be able to see the actual formation of matter from vibration and frequency.

We would literally be able to see creation happening?

Indeed. That discovery being made manifest is near.

Well that's cool, but we got off subject.

Actually, we didn't. You asked what was here before matter. We are showing you that even now, matter as you think of it does not exist. The formation of your universe came when desire sent out a massive wave of potentiality . . .

Well, where did this wave come from?

It came from the consciousness of the one. The desire created the new space of potential. From this creation, the frequencies were formed and bonded together. They then formed vibrations. The vibrations took "shape," as you would say, and the universe was born. You see, you do not yet think of vibrations or frequencies as "solid." Indeed, they are as real a part of an object as the atoms that comprise them. For what constitutes an atom? And what of the space between the atoms? Atoms are in fact the "visual" representation of the frequency/vibration potentiality.

Whoa. That's a new concept. Care to elaborate?

Everything is energy, is it not?

Yes. You've said that a few times.

So then, what makes a piece of wood different from a blade of grass? What makes you different from either?

Well, with regard to the second question, I would say consciousness.

This is not correct. There is no separation other than that which you perceive.

Okay. You'll have to really help me, because it sounds like you're saying that basically, I'm the same thing as a blade of grass.

Your ego doesn't like that comparison, does it? You are consciousness. You are human. How then, can you be the same as a blade of grass?

I have a feeling you're going to tell me.

Yep. The answer is: You're the same. Everything is energy. Your consciousness is not your body, yet your body is a manifestation of your spirit, which is consciousness. So then, at the level of no separation—and we are not talking of the spiritual notion, we are speaking of beyond the atomic region —there is nothing that distinguishes you from anything other than your own perception. Your ego is a mechanism of this perception. Obviously, you have chosen to come here and experience being an individualized energy, yet your individuality is just an illusion. Science is beginning to discover what will inevitably lead to this remembrance on a mass scale: all are one.

Okay, so relate that to vibration/frequency potentiality.

Well, if a wave of potential with unlimited possibilities goes out into a system of consciousness such as yours, where beliefs and self-imposed limitation come into play, your beliefs will guide your frequencies to create in one way or the other. It is the story of manifestation. You have a desire, the desire expresses itself, and you manifest. Sometimes you manifest the exact thing for which you have asked. Sometimes, you manifest a variation of your desire, and sometimes you manifest more desire. It is important for you to realize that even in "not manifesting" your desire, you are still manifesting. Often you do not see something show up; it slips under your radar, and you think "well then, I must not be a creator." That is not the case. You are always creating. You are always the creator.

Now, what you have manifested has come from where?

most would say: "It was made in a factory," or "I bought it," or "It came from the earth."

I buy that answer.

In actuality, it has come from Source. And what may have started as polymers and aluminum in some factory has now become your new car. However, where did those polymers come from? How is steel forged? Scientifically, you can trace the material in your world all the way back to its elemental form. What we are here to tell you with regard to vibration/frequency potentiality is that at some point, the template—or DNA for these elements was chosen by thought and desire. Remember, everything is happening at the same time. Therefore, a material may be discovered today and put to use in a new way, but the idea and desire for that material, or its potential, sprang forth in the beginning when all things were conceived. Therefore, desire starts the wave, and it goes forth as manifestation occurs—long before the atoms are formed, or the DNA or its material makeup is decided upon. The vibrations and frequency then move into alignment accordingly. Have we lost you?

I don't think so. Basically, desire begins the creation process, and as the creation narrows into specific potentialities, the frequencies and vibrations form accordingly. To use the example of the harp, as creation grows the strings tune themselves to their respective notes. So, at the microcosmic level, everything is the same frequency/vibration, and for lack of a better explanation, as desire is focused upon, the resonance of the vibrations and frequencies begin to change so that they can make up whatever physical or non-physical aspect they are to become.

Very good. Maybe we should change places.

Not when I still have questions. Like, is this how the universe was created?

Indeed. It also explains what you would call evolution. We'd like to point out that when something evolves, it changes—as does its story. We say again, in order to usher in the greatest change, you must be willing to let go of all that you have thought. That's not to say what you've thought is right or wrong, but it is a story. It is a definition, and as long as you are defined, you cannot be undefined, and your story cannot change.

Now, to understand fully how the manifestation, the expansion, and the unfolding occur, we must examine your beliefs. Before we look to your conscious mind, however, we must look at the polarities that exist within the vibrations, within the frequencies, and indeed within your consciousness.

Chapter Seven

Creation and the Perception of Polarity

You can't create abundance from the vibration of lack. However, lack and abundance are two sides of the same coin. In your terms, you would call them "polarities," but we'd like to be quick to point out that there are no polarities. Polarities are a creation of your own mind.

Then, wouldn't that mean they DO exist?

In your mind. We're going to get into "knowing" and what we really mean when we say that later on. However, at this point, know that if you perceive polarity, you will experience it as a reality. That does not mean it is truly present. You could put red lenses over your eyes and perceive everything you see as red. Does that make the world red?

Well, it seems to me that it would. If my perception is what creates...

It's not your perception that creates reality, it's you. Don't confuse the two. Yes, you perceive redness (in this example), but you're also able to remove the lenses and see what is "actually" there. In other words, you saw red because your perception told you there was red. You trusted your perception. You knew it to be right. You knew that you were seeing red. Why you were seeing red, was of no consequence. Whether you consciously knew the lenses were there or not, you saw red, and thus, everything was red. Were you to remove the lenses, your perception would change. The surface appearance does not change, yet it now *looks* different. And the important thing to always know is: you are always free to remove whatever lenses you may be wearing.

And back to lack and abundance?

We never left it, but since we have given you the answer before examining the question, let's look at what you call "polarity," and how this idea might work in this context: Within the energy of abundance, there is the choice for lack. Within "I want it" is the choice of "I don't want it," and as you move forward in releasing your stories, you may find that you are experiencing some of the past—your past patterns may reemerge. This is simply what you would call "the polarity" that exists within the vibration of letting go of your stories, and is the vibration of not letting go. In order to neutralize "the polarities" in your perception and move into total choice, we ask that you move into total love, total trust, and total harmony—for harmony is living without polarities, it is living in eternal choice. When you can know with all of your being, then you may choose with all of your being, and what you call "polarity" will cease to exist because there will be no room for doubt or struggle.

When this is achieved, you are at the zero point - the point of total being - where you are always free to choose. You become an active creator rather than simply creating on autopilot or creating based on wishy-washy wants that are in opposition to vibrations of your core beliefs.

We're talking about movement on a vibrational level. How do I do that?

Yes, we are talking about concepts that are strange, possibly foreign, to human nature; yet you do it just as you do anything else. The first step in reaching the balance is simply to want the balance. Now, if you vibrationally find yourself struggling to want the balance, simply claim "I Am Self-Love." This will shift everything into divine love and allow you to move into the zero point of energetic choice. We say "move you into energetic choice" not because it is moving you, but you yourself, through claiming your own expression, through your own vibrations, are plotting in the sequence that will release you from any other "program" (thoughts, beliefs, etc) your mind/energy may be running.

Now we have touched on lack and abundance (and lack and abundance are at their core simply the altered frequencies of love). Originally, you understood lack and abundance to be polarities just as you perceived love and fear to be polarity. Creation/Non Creation, sickness/ health, lack/abundance, all of these things are expressions of the same energy. It is only through perception, identification, and judgment that they become an empowered "other" energy. It is all simply an allowance or disallowance of love. For sometimes, we fear that which we are, and in a place of fear, we will activate the vibration of fear.

I thought you just said everything was love?

Yes. It would be the same to say: "Sometimes, we do not love that which we are, and in a place of non-love, we create and allow the further exploration of not loving our Self."

Oh. Wow. Okay. I get that.

Look at it this way, if you are trying to create, if you are having the desire for something, and a part of you fears that something, you will activate vibrations that say, "Bring it on!" and vibrations that would sooner die than get the thing for which you are asking.

Been there, done that. (Pause) We've talked a lot about vibration. What's the difference between vibration and frequency?

That's a good question. Vibrations are made up of frequencies. Within the vibration of wanting, there is also the frequency of not wanting. Picture it as a rainbow. The rainbow, for the sake of this example, is the total unit of color. The rainbow would then represent the vibration. The individual colors within the spectrum of that vibration represent frequency. Now, as the frequencies within the vibration change, so does the vibration.

You may be in a vibration of happiness, and then, you may find yourself moving from a vibration of happiness into one of joy, or from happiness into despondency, and what has happened is that frequencies within the vibration have altered. We feel it is important for you to know that they have altered because of your direction. Your vibrations and their frequencies are a direct reflection of choice. So then, it is not a difficult stretch for your mind to realize that your vibrations are made up of hundreds, thousands of frequencies, and within the vibration of you as a singular energy are millions of other vibrations composed of multiple frequencies.

Now, hold on to your quantum hats, because this may get tricky. Frequencies are composed of vibrations.

What? How can vibrations be made up of frequencies, and frequencies be made of vibrations?

Again, it may be difficult to get your head around it, but let go. You will see. Think of the frequencies as harp strings. As you adjust a single string, the whole instrument and its total resonance is changed—the instrument here being creation, which is the ultimate vibration. Now we have said to you that everything is a vibration within a vibration within a vibration, etc., so on the smallest scale, the frequencies make up the vibrations, but those vibrations then serve as the frequencies or subunits for other more inclusive vibrations, and so on and so forth. Like the Mandelbrot Set you mentioned earlier.

So, creation starts with frequency?

No. Creation starts with being. Being then creates desires, which creates the waves of potentiality from which you will choose, or not choose, or both (which you will perceive as polarity). It comes down to this: Where choice is fully present, there can be no polarity.

What if I am choosing polarity?

And aren't you?

Oh.

Yeah. Get it?

I feel like I just got called out, lol.

Well, in a way, you did, but only because you chose to (laughter). You see, when you choose something with all of your being, there is no polarity. Take for example: love. If you can see love everywhere, in all situations, there will be only love.

How could I choose to see love in war?

Are you at war?

Not personally, but . . .

Then why would you consciously focus on war?

Okay, well talk to the person who may have read that statement who has suffered abuse or who is at war in a foreign country.

Can you feel yourself becoming offended at the information we are bringing forth?

Absolutely. I really feel kind of angry and pissed off all of the sudden, and I don't really know why... I just am.

Partly because what we just said leaves no room for suffering or righteousness. These things that we're talking about, abuse and war, they're parts of your story - both individually and collectively. If there were suddenly peace on earth, and everybody who had ever wronged you in your eyes came forward and deeply apologized, what would you do?

You wouldn't know where to start. You'd be even more pissed off (as you say), and the reason is because you're not letting go. You're choosing to hold on to a story that does not serve you in any way other than to keep you plugged in and charged with the same energy that creates war and abuse in your self and in your world. As you said the other day, "would you rather be happy or right?" In this case, you would rather be right. How can you be right, if there is no wrong? Therefore, war MUST be wrong. Judgment. Abuse MUST be wrong. Judgment. You see we're back to that. Let go of your righteousness and your judgment. You have just provided a wonderful example of what leaving your knowing looks like. Better yet, you left for what you would term "a good reason." You see, you can own your own creations. You can look at your own life and say, "well, I created suffering there, and I forgive myself because I didn't know I was creating it," but can you release the world? Can you allow the world its own experience? When you can do that, when you can look out and know that what you are seeing is just a part of the whole that is experiencing its own reality for a vast myriad of reasons, and you can refrain from casting judgment (judging an experience, or a circumstance, or even judging yourself for NOT judging something), then you can be in the world and not of it.

Wow. I can see that.

Yes, but there will be those who struggle here. Their choice to struggle is as valid as they create it to be. However, there is no need for struggle. You hear it all the time: "It's all good." We've heard you say it. IT really simply IS—no judgment. Whatever IT is, IT is always a creation, a choice.

Now, we wish to make one other point as we have been discussing what you perceive to be polarities within the one energy. We want for you to know that compassion and sympathy are just as damaging as the energy of war and abuse. For if there is a desire to experience compassion, there is the desire for an experience that will bring about compassion. The same is true for sympathy. Do you follow?

Yeah, but isn't there a difference between "healthy" and "unhealthy" compassion? Like, isn't it good to have compassion for the poor as opposed to say getting violently ill so someone will take compassion on me, or even experiencing poverty in order to gain compassion?

You've answered your own question. If you are compassionate for the poor, you are feeding the same energy that creates poverty . . .

Whoa-whoa-whoa. Say what?

We will use the example of a penny: compassion for the poor and poverty are two sides of the same coin. A coin may not be the optimal illustration for every example because some subjects may have several sides, but the idea is the same. If there is present the desire to experience being compassionate, a situation must be created wherein that desire can be fulfilled.

Shit. So by giving money to the poor, you're saying I'm creating poverty?

No. You may give money to the poor. You may shelter the homeless. You may council the blind. You may care for the wounded, but do so knowing that each one of you creates your own life—literally. Don't pass a homeless person and judge yourself good for giving them money or bad for not giving them money. Know that they are sovereign creators just as you are. If your desire is to give, and their desire is to receive, wonderful. You are a vibrational match for the creation of a shared experience. If they wish to be passed over, and you pass them over, wonderful. If either one of you are unclear in your choice, you'll experience perceptually a polarity.

What does that mean?

We'll use an example: Let's say you are struggling with your sense of worth, and you pass a beggar on the street. You look at this person who is physically asking for money, and you say, "No." Within this scenario, there are a myriad of things that could be happening. The beggar may be showing up as a reflection of your views on the universe. Maybe you believe you are unworthy of having what you ask for, and so you have created this situation so that you may see that you are both the beggar who is asking, and the rich man saying "no!" Maybe you feel you have been taken advantage of and that you are constantly saying "yes" when you wish you could say "no." In that case, you could have created this opportunity to allow yourself to say "no" in a place you see as safe, or to *freely* give where there is no perceived pressure. On the other hand, the homeless person may hold conflicting beliefs about their worth, so some people will give them money, and others will walk on by. There are literally thousands of scenarios and "beliefs" that could play out here, but the overall principal of creation holds true.

In other words, I can only create for myself, right?

This is true for all energy.

But if we are all one-energy, shouldn't I help whenever and wherever I can?

You "help" by choosing love.

So we're back to "I am Self-Love?"

Yes, but let us explain. We've said that you are all individualized expressions of Source Energy, and we've discussed how creation occurs. Can you see that by releasing judgment, you free everything?

What do you mean?

Can you allow that experiences are neither good nor bad, they just are? And they <u>are</u> because they are the answer to a desire that was born and called forth into experience? If you can know that everything is Source, and that you are the only one who can create your life, can you allow that the same is true for all energy?

When you can KNOW this, you can truly stand unshaken in the midst of an earthquake.

Why the emphasis on know?

If all that is exists outside of what you call time and space—what some refer to as the Akashic Records—is it not too far of a jump to realize that not knowing is also just a perception?

Right. Basically, I don't know anything until I allow myself to know.

Yes. Everything there is to know is knowable in the now, for where else would it be? Now is all there is. If thoughts are frequencies and waves, are they birthed from the molecules of a book, or the sound waves of a voice? Of course not.

Information is information. Knowledge is knowledge. You can open up and know everything you need to know right now.

What do you mean?

Well, most people believe what they believe because of what they know. Take this for example: If someone is born into this existence with the template "I am an abused child," yet their biggest belief is "I don't know I am Source who creates all," they'll continue to believe they are somehow abused by the universe, by themselves, and by others, until they KNOW that they are Source and can author any change to this template they wish. What they know, has allowed their belief to shift, yet your belief was in direct relation to what they knew. So long as they did not know, their beliefs would have always mirrored that lack of knowing.

Another example: How are you receiving the information for this book?

. . . Oh.

Yeah. "Oh!" You opened yourself up to knowing - first to knowing it was possible to channel information, and then to knowing you could do it, and now you are doing it. What do you think that is? You're opening up to a larger part of what is available to you now – a larger part of YOU!

Wow. That's deep. It makes sense though.

This conversation veered off a little bit from our discussion about creation, frequency, waves. If we've answered your question sufficiently, we'd like to move back to that.

Please. That was really great. By all means, let's continue.

Well, we were talking about your perception of polarity in the outer world and how that outer world comes into being. In order to understand the outer, one must understand where and how it begins. Think of Source here as a giant spectrum of light projecting unlimited potential at all times. Your thoughts form the waves of light that guide your consciousness into this stream of potentiality to create manifestation. The waves then form the frequencies, which form the vibrations, which form the frequencies, etc. which creates or brings in the outer experience.

So my desire creates a wave of potential, into which the frequencies gather. The frequencies then form vibrations, and as I expand—in desire, physicality, and consciousness—those vibrations become the building blocks of other frequencies, which then create more vibrations... or in other words, as within, so without, right?

Yes! So you can see how important it is to keep your own house in order, so to speak.

How does all of this relate to "I am Self-Love?"

Self-Love is that perfect place of no judgment, no story, just pure being. It is the experience of knowing that you are loved by a universe of unlimited potential, and in turn, that you love your Self—for everything is Source. Vibrationally, this addresses any frequencies that you may or may not know you are creating (i.e. a belief, a pattern, something stored genetically, etc).

You know energy creates, and everything is energy. By claiming Self-Love, you are tuning not just the individual frequency - the smallest level of vibrations composed of frequencies - but you are literally changing the frequencies within every single layer of the vibration that is you - all the way up to the totality of consciousness: the one consciousness. These vibrations are the vibrations that allow you to manifest that which you desire. They are literally the vibrations of the manifestation of creation, and as you claim the frequency, these vibrations expand. More frequencies are then added, and thus more

116

potentialities are added to your creation. The potential for more new thought arises as you expand.

One way to choose to enter a state of divine love (a state of fully embracing and loving your self), is to recognize that you are not your stories. You are not your feelings. You are not your emotions. You are pure source energy. You are pure or self love. To recognize this and to choose to claim it as who you are is to move into the allowance of all that is. By loving your self, you're not only making the choice to balance your vibrations, you are making the choice to come forward for yourself - to come forward *as* yourself - in a new creation.

When we talk to you about fear, intention, releasing your stories, and so on, we want you to know these aren't hurdles to creation; they're merely steps in a process. Life is always a process: steps of releasing, steps of growth, and steps of evolving into that which you are.

So what then is Self-Love and how is it different?

We say "Self-Love," but we want you to know that Self-Love and Divine Love are the same thing, because that which you are is divine, and that which you are is pure source energy. If you don't know you are divine love, feel into love, and choose to choose. Choose to know, and choose to allow. Choose to move through your fears, into your intention, release your story, unify with your spirit, and expand your consciousness into knowing that *you are* divine love.

When you can love yourself, you're not only focused on love, but you're focused on the divine, and what you focus on, you will create. In this case, you'll create more divine love. You will create the life you want. You'll create it, because you love yourself to give yourself the keys to the kingdom. True Self/Divine Love is loving yourself and experiencing yourself as Source experiences you, because you are the same.

We'll spin it this way: who are the people you wish to give things to in your life?

People I love.

Right. It brings you pleasure and in some cases a sense of worth to be able to provide for the people you love. Now, many people today have been taught not to fully love themselves. They've been taught through books or religion or society that they come later: God and country first, then others, then, if there's any time left, the self. In reality, people have to put themselves first. This might seem like a selfish idea to many, but it isn't, because in divine love, you're able to come forward for yourself in all ways. When you can do that and come forward as the spiritual source you are, you can then come forward for others as the God, as the creator, that you are.

I have a pretty good understanding of that, but what's going on vibrationally when I claim, "I am Self-Love?"

Vibrationally, the frequencies come into alignment and enable the creation of manifestation and the creation of divine love. Again, when you focus on Self Love, you are releasing everything else about you: who and what you think you are. When you can open up and simply be the love that you are, your resonance will change, meaning your vibrations will change, and in turn, what you create will change. It's as if you were attempting to paint a rainbow using nothing but the color blue, and we've given you the key to access the other colors. In becoming divine love, Self Love, you are expanding your color palette. With many colors to choose from, your creation not only becomes easier, but you're able to do more with it.

So it really all comes down to "I have to love myself?"

Yes, and for some people this will be the most difficult choice they can make. So around choosing to let go of the reasons, to let go of the stories, excuses as to why you do not love yourself, choosing to let go of the baggage, to let go of the teachings, and choosing to let go of the feelings, claim "I am Self-Love."

In claiming Self-Love, not only does your resonance change, not only does your vibration change, but your "chakras" (as you call them)—of which there are more than seven—also begin to open and expand. The more you love yourself, the more you *allow* Your Self, and the more potential there is, the more Source Energy comes in and flows. The more you expand, the more your energy expands, and the more that which you are, Source Energy, can come forward into your creation.

So what do my chakras have to do with it?

That's another good question. Most people don't think of the chakras with relation to creation, but within your system, the chakras help regulate the flow of energy at your behest. And through your chakras, different ideas are formed and are spun into your energy. As they open and spin and expand, the capacity for new thoughts increases.

And as it increases and I move into a state of balance and Self-Love, all that I am, all that we are, continues to unfold in a more limitless way?

Yes, that is correct. There is nothing - that is to say there is no thing - which love will not overcome. We'll show you a few examples in the chapters to come of specific frequencies you can tune in order to create the "you" (and the world) that you consciously desire.

Chapter Eight

Fear of Creation

The first frequency we wish to address is the fear of creation. We want to start here because this is the first in the sequence of frequencies or thought patterns that, when balanced, allow you to manifest what you've called forth from Source. Obviously, your entire creation is made up of many frequencies, but we want to specifically address those that specifically pertain to manifestation.

All right, let's talk fear of creation.

As we explain the frequencies, you'll see their multidimensionality and their function within the different levels of manifestation. For example, if you want to create anything on this physical plain, this fear frequency must be balanced with regard to what you want to create. However, it must also be balanced on the larger scale of fearing yourself as the creator that you are.

If you fear yourself as creation, then according to the degree of that fear, you'll do one of two things:

You will not create what you've set out to bring forth. Or,

you will create it in a way that is not harmonious with your desire.

Within these two scenarios are the explanations to the often-asked questions of "Why?" "Why did this thing happen to me?" "Why does my world look like this, and why does this keep happening to me?!"

It's also the answer to "why" there is war. It is the answer to all of those questions and many more.

That's pretty big

It's huge! Within your desire to expand is fear. When activated and/or focused upon, this fear will be an undercurrent in all of your creation efforts. Taking the example of war, we would say that there are a multitude of fears at play— ultimately it boils down to the fear of creation, and we will show you what that looks like.

Let's examine this idea with regards to war between religions. In a situation like this, there is a belief in a creator other than self. This creator often has specific things He or She has commanded his or her followers to do. There is a clear cut set of beliefs, ideals, social constructs, and values set forth. This causes war not only between religion, but it also causes war within the Self.

How so?

If someone believes whole-heartedly in a creator being outside of the self, and they also believe in an after-life ruled over by this creator (or even that this current existence is ruled by that creator), then any thought or action that comes about in opposition to the aforementioned beliefs and ideals creates a serious problem. The self is literally threatened any time a desire forms that is outside of the set parameters of the creator being. This life is threatened as well as the next. In this scenario, there is only one way to God, and that is to do what God says. Therefore, anyone who doesn't share your beliefs not only opposes you, but they also oppose God – and how DARE they?! Some take this to an extreme and believe that because another does not believe in their God, they're then an enemy of that God and an enemy of all of that God's followers. The bottom line is, if you're right, and you have a mandate from your God, (that which you believe to be the source of all creation), you will have created the ultimate excuse for your actions be they war, oppression, violence, etc, because these aren't really your actions, they are commandments from God.

I get that, but I don't see the fear of creation at play here.

Remember that by simply being here you are in self-creation. If you knew that and embraced that - and truly embraced all of creation as your own, would you be in fear of any other?

Well, yeah. Some people are just crazy.

Just like that, you've given your creative power over to those you perceive as crazy. If you truly knew that you were the creator of all that you experience, you would not be afraid of anyone, even the "crazies." You would know without a doubt that no one could do anything to you, and that if you found yourself in an unlikable or dangerous situation, you would know that you created it through the activation of fear, and you would know how to create the change you wished to experience.

How do you explain that to people who have lost loved ones in wars or attacks?

You don't. For no one has been lost. This is why we've come forth: So you can better know your union with Source. No one "goes" anywhere with regard to a finite resting place. You always exist.

And for those who don't believe that?

Their suffering will eventually awaken them to self-creation. This is why we have asked you to release your emotional attachments. They block you from the truth, and the truth is: only you create your life.

This is why it is so important to give up our stories?

Yes. There will be people will choose not to give them up who, and that's okay. We're here for the consciousness that wishes to move now. Again, no one will be left behind. No one will be lost, but on a large scale, consciousness wants to move, and we're here to show how to make this shift.

From a philosophical standpoint, I can see what you are saying. If I know that I am my own creator, then nothing is outside of my influence, but shit happens. How do I . . .

Love. Love yourself. Love your neighbor. Love all. Many people reading these words will be feeling just as much resistance as you are. As you

127

feel this resistance, claim "I Am Self-Love." If you find that you are not in trust yet, tell yourself, I AM Love. You are safe where you are. These feelings that are coming up are a result of your fear of and around creation. We mentioned there were other ways for this to show up, and resistance is one of them. You're taught that resistance is your intuition warning you that something is wrong, but the only thing "wrong" is that you don't know your power. These feelings are a reminder that you don't quite know that which you've set out to know. It's just fear coming up to be released, so release.

By claiming Self-Love?

You're not just claiming it, you're telling the energy, "I Am" that which I have claimed. "I Am Self-Love. I am the love of myself as divine, Source energy. I am experiencing myself both as the giver and receiver of love."

Can you give me a few more examples of how the fear of creation might look?

Sure. You've experienced what were diagnosed as panic attacks, right?

Yep.

And do you understand how those were in part forms of severe resistance?

Sort of.

(Playfully) There's no sort of about it. Another part of you, which you were not consciously aware of, was asking for this information, and as we made contact and you began to expand, you "freaked out," as you might say. It's important to state that this didn't need to happen, but here, your energy (in the form of old belief systems) felt attacked by your own expansion of energy. You were holding so tightly to your stories, that as more of you came in to love you, you physically freaked out because you were in fear of all this love.

That reminds me of that great Marianne Williamson quote about how it's not our darkness that we most fear, it's our light.

She was right.

But back to your panic attacks, all illness is a form of fear. You might not be able to understand it as such, but it is a manifestation of the frequency of fear. Remember, everything you experience in life is frequency and vibration, and so everything, while being the one energy, has its own vibration and frequency. Therefore, your life could be looked upon as a series of subjects: health, love, relationships, career, etc. These subjects then have a relation to each other. For example, there is the subject of relationships, but that does not just mean only your physical relationship with your partner. It includes your relationships to all people and things, including other subjects, and their relation to each other.

Holy crap. That's a lot of vibrations.

It sure is. This is why Self-Love is so great. It gives you the ability to direct all of your energy - and all of the frequencies within that energy. You've always had the power to direct, but this allows you to focus and direct on a massive scale.

This may sound silly, but this explains "miracles" in a pretty cool way. It makes sense. I mean, if you can totally allow and direct, there's really no limit, is there?

Nope. There are physical aspects to your reality, physical laws, and most have come here to experience life in this plain with these limitations. Yet, a very small portion of consciousness has chosen to have the experience of expanding beyond these laws.

The fear then arises because to expand beyond these "laws" of physics requires one to fully know and own their creatorship, and if I own mine, what will I do? What will others who do not yet know theirs think of me? What will they do to me?" You see, they cannot "do" anything to you. These fears, however, are the blueprint for remembering who you are and then suffering because of it. It's the idea that if people know how great you truly are, they'll come in droves to take you down – because who are you to be so great? So again, you see the role fear plays.

Wow. That's amazing.

Very much wow.

So what are the exact words I would use in claiming this formula?

You don't even need words – which actually brings us to the second part of this blueprint: the frequency of intention.

So... Next chapter?

Next chapter.

Chapter Nine

Intention

Before we begin this chapter, let's claim Self-Love.

I Am Self-Love... that felt good.

Good. Now, you've heard a lot about "intention" over the past few years with regard to creation. One side says intention is everything, while the other comes back with, "Okay then, get out of that chair by intention alone. You can't! You can only decide to move, and then execute that decision."

Both sides are right. In order to remove yourself from the chair, you must first intend to move. You must then keep this intention as it becomes physical action. Do you understand?

Yes. So, the action of getting up is the physical manifestation of the intention to get up?

Yes. Think of it in terms of wave and potentiality. The physical action itself is the realized potential or extension of the wave of intention and desire. You can have intentions that you don't act upon, but what hinders the action is the frequency of the intention.

With a balanced frequency, intention becomes action. Therefore, we move through the fear of creation and into intention.

That's it?

Not quite. There's another question with regard to intention that you have yet to ask.

And that would be . . . (Pause) *"How do I know my intention?"*

Correct. How *do* you know your intention?

Ummm. I asked you first.

(Laughing) Okay. Your mind tells you that you know your intention by what you consciously want. However, this doesn't leave room for the subconscious mind or for the energetic belief systems that are at play beyond your perception.

I think I know where this is going now.

There are many ways for you to tap into your own energy. You communicate with your inner self in a variety of ways including meditation and dreams. However, there are ways of speaking to yourself (both your specific energy and the energy of all) that most people aren't aware of. There is one way in particular that requires no training and nothing other than the use of your own body. We've chosen to discuss this within the subtext of intention because not only does it allow you to truly know the energy and thoughts you are holding, but it also requires your intention: the intention to truly know Thy Self.

Often times, you may want an answer that makes sense in a limited way or one that will validate either your beliefs or those of your culture. Get out of your head and trust the universe. Trust Source. You may think one thing, but energetically, you may be holding a desire or belief that is completely different or even completely contrary to what you're asking for, and this energy may be subverting your conscious intention.

Now, this practice will require that you stand up (if you are unable to stand, we will list an alternative method later.). For some of you, this will work automatically. For others, you might need to balance some energy. Here is the exercise:

Stand up straight. Open up to your higher self. Know that you are completely safe. Ask that you be shown your yes movement. At this point, you will lean a certain way. You may even feel as if you are being pushed. Don't worry about how large your motion is or which direction you move as there is no right or wrong here. At this point, we just want to get your "yes." If you are having trouble, it is because of resistance – be it a belief sustem, fear, whatever. Self-Love will remove the resistance and any other limitations if you allow it. Claim Self Love while choosing to move into this experience.

Okay. I lean backwards. That's my "yes."

Very Good. We would like to remind the reader that they may move in a different direction. The direction is not important, only

135

that you have a clear "yes" and "no." Now say "show me my no."

I lean forward.

You now have a very important tool for tapping in to your energy. Remember, that is all this it is. There's nothing to be afraid of. There's no outside force moving against you or through. You're simply tapping in to yourself. Your energy is able to move you like a leaf in the wind.

So it's using the body like a pendulum?

Indeed. We mentioned that often times your mind will tell you "Yes, this is correct," while your energy disagrees. An example would be a person who says with regard to a promotion, "Yes, I want this," while they energetically hold the belief that "I am not good enough, and I don't belong." This creates a separation between their desire and their ability to manifest said desire. They consciously want a thing, have the intention, but their whole energy cannot support its manifestation.

A way to then use this tool would be to ask yourself, "There are frequencies to be balanced around this subject or any other subject which will affect the manifestation of what I am wanting?" We say "any other subject" because often times, there will be a frequency to balance from another subject that in your mind is totally unrelated. If you get your yes, simply claim, "I Am Self-Love." Sometimes there are layers of collapsed belief, and based on your own energetic beliefs, you may or may not need to claim this more than once in order to balance all levels.

How will I know if there are layers to balance?

Each time you claim Self-Love, you may ask, "Are those frequencies 100% balanced?" If you get a "no," it is important to ask whether or not you want them to balance. If you get that you're resistant to balancing certain frequencies, direct yourself to choose to balance. Direct yourself to choose healing. If you get a "yes," and the frequencies still don't balance, ask yourself "Do I have permission to do this work?" Remember that you are your own God. If you do not get that you have permission, it is only because a part of your energy is either not wanting to move forward, or is holding itself back by giving its creation away to someone else. You are in charge of all of your energy. It is all yours, and it will respond to your direction when you so choose.

Now, if you wish, you can ask for discernment by stating, "Is it is really about this subject that I am now holding in my mind?" Other questions to ask your self would include:

1. Am I balanced?

2. Am I unbalanced?

3. Do I want the highest answer?

4. Do I want to move forward?

5. Am I allowing myself to move forward?

6.	Is there anything in my way that I perceive is not myself?

What does that mean?

In other words, "Is there a part of me holding on to someone else's definition of me." Sometimes people energetically feel like someone or something is controlling them. Take for example the child who feels like they can't move forward and truly express who they are without letting down their parents. The child is at choice, but it feels like the parent is holding the child back. It's all about perception.

What about number three? I thought there wasn't a "highest" answer.

There isn't. And there is. If you are going to take a trip, and you want to get there in the quickest amount of time possible, would you rather take a road packed with traffic and slow moving vehicles, or would you rather take a highway with high speeds and low traffic?

Highway, hands down.

That's what we mean by "highest answer." We use "highest" here meaning that your mind isn't meddling and your ego is out of the way.

Again, These questions are merely for discernment. Your intention is to always allow everything to be in balance, and therefore you should not need to refer to these questions. It may seem like a lot to learn right now, but once you get the language, it is just as natural as speaking. You will not think twice about any of it.

Let it be your intention every time you claim Self-Love to claim it on behalf of all energy in all time and space. Remember, you are physically focused here in this plane, but you exist in many, many places. It is our desire that you claim Self-Love on behalf of ALL that you are.

You mentioned other ways to test energy.

Yes. You may communicate with your energy in a variety of other ways. We would like to specifically mention muscle testing and pendulum use. Most muscle testing involves using a second person; therefore we would recommend using a pendulum simply because you can do it on your own. Since you use a pendulum, would you like to describe its use?

Sure. A pendulum, first of all, has no power. It is like a phone. It's just a means of communication. It can be anything from a necklace, to a crystal on a chain, to a tea bag, or even a paper clip on the end of a string. Anything with weight at the end should work fine. I hold mine with my index finger, thumb, and middle finger. Basically, you use it in the same manner that is described above. You get your "yes" and your "no" movements and work from there. My yes is a counter-clockwise circle. My "no" is a clockwise circle. Did I miss anything?

That was fine. We would like to add that the questions should pertain to the now moment--- that is to say the questions should be about what you are creating now. For example, you may want to create a new relationship. You would not say, "I'm going to meet someone tonight" and look for a "yes" or "no." You would check the statement, "My current energy is open to receiving and creating the experience of a relationship now." As you progress if you feel yourself close down with regard to your openness, you would simply claim "I Am Self-Love."

Remember, you are claiming Self-Love and expanding, and as you expand, so do your frequencies of love. You have a relationship to your creation. It is an ongoing process. As you create, new desire forms with new frequencies. Once you have set your intention and made the choice to expand into the manifestation of your desires, all you have to do is trust.

And then what?

Let's turn the page and find out!

Chapter Ten

From Trusting to Allowing

One of the easiest ways to move into a vibration of joyful knowing and manifestation is to fully trust every moment and every thing.

Because of The Law of Attraction?

Because of all of it. Trust the Universe.

"Don't separate." I got it, but I gotta say, "trust the Universe" sounds kind of nebulous.

Because you don't trust the Universe.

I'm sitting here talking to you, aren't I?

You trust this experience—of having a conversation with Source—now, because you know it to be true, but you had to work your way up to it.

If you were staring at a painting of a giant red dot and someone came in and in complete sincerity said, "That's not the way you draw a blue square," you might look at them and say something sarcastic or completely ignore them, but would you at any point say, "Oh my God, you're right!"

No. I wouldn't. I might wonder what was in their coffee (or maybe where I could get some), but I wouldn't really pay much attention to them.

Well, to be honest, whatever it is that's in their coffee, you're drinking it every day. You wake up and sift through your own criticisms and judgments and you allow them to get a hold of your thoughts and feelings, and these things keep you from trusting who you really are and everything that comes into your life. It's kind of like drinking to your own doubt."

How did we get from "The red-dot painting" to the non-trust double latte?

By not trusting the flow. In your life, you have events that occur: sometimes you perceive these as large events like marriage or divorce, and sometimes you view them as small, like stubbing your toe on your way out the door.

Which hurts by the way.

How long does the physical pain last?

Maybe a couple of seconds, sometimes longer depending on . . . Well, I was going to say "depending on how long I focus on it."

Yet that one event, those few seconds, can literally ruin your entire day, and that ruined day can ruin your entire week. That week . . .

No, I get that, but how does all of this relate back to trust?

In the moment you stubbed your toe, you had the choice to do everything from curse and holler and throw things to not reacting at all. Now, we wouldn't tell you to stifle a real emotion.

What do you mean a "real emotion?"

We'll get there. Just trust where we're going.

Say you feel like crying, but you hold that emotion back and say, "I'm not going to let this stubbed toe affect my day. I must stay positive!" This isn't going to help anything. In fact, it's creating more distrust because you are vibrationally telling yourself something along the lines of "My feelings are bad" or "I must not express certain feelings if I want to gain a certain outcome." You must trust whatever happens, all of it. In a balanced place of trust, you might simply say, "Ouch. That hurt. I'm going to sit here and send my toe some love."

Okay. Really?!? "I'm going to send some love to my toe? ...Seriously?

Well, since love is the glue that holds the universe together (as well as your toe), it's the right salve to apply. But let's try another track.

Think of Source as a giant conglomeration of every single radio station there is, was, or will ever be. You are an extension of Source, and your extremities are extensions of all that you are. Tune your entire self to love and broadcast that and the universe will completely "have your back" as you say.

You had an interesting experience with a flip-flop last summer. Care to share?

Ah. The white flip-flop thing. Yeah.

What happened?

Well, I had a dream a couple nights before I left to visit my parents for a few weeks. In the dream, I was driving my mom's car—which is a super awesome Lexus convertible—and I was going through a stoplight down the street from their house. And a big SUV ran through the light and nailed me. The car spun around. The glass all broke, and I remember saying to myself, "I'm wearing the brown shirt I just bought and my cargo shorts. This must be real." The last thing I remember was noticing all the blood on my shirt and then noticing my shoes. I was wearing a pair of white flip-flops.

And so what happened?

Cut to a week or so later, and I was running out the door to meet a friend for lunch. I over slept and was running late, so I threw some clothes on and ran out the door still half asleep. I jumped in my mom's car and peeled out of the driveway. I wasn't even all the way down the driveway when I realized I was wearing the brown shirt, cargo pants, and white flip-flops – the exact outfit from my dream. I stopped dead in my tracks, put the car in reverse and backed up the driveway, ran in and grabbed another pair of flip-flops.

How long did this take?

It took maybe two minutes. And the whole time I was thinking, "I'm so late, but I'd rather be late and paranoid than bleed all over my new shirt."

144

Well, as dumb and paranoid as I felt running back inside just to change flip flops, I'm sure glad I did it. About a mile from the house, I passed an accident at the exact spot from my dream. A black SUV had plowed into another car. The accident wasn't more than a few minutes old as the police weren't even there (and the accident happened about a mile and a half from the station).

So you felt like you had been protected?

Absolutely.

You felt like the Universe "had your back?"

Of course.

Yet, you get pissed off when you stub your toe or when a certain relationship ends?

How is that even in the same ballpark? That's totally different.

No. It's not. It's always you, and it's always according to what you really want and what your beliefs are.

What do you mean?

Let's look at this with regard to relationships. You recently had a relationship change.

That's a nice way of putting it.

How would you put it?

No, no. If I take the bait and blame or say something like, "She's crazy" or "I got dumped" or use any of those excuses. . .

(Pause) Oh.

(Laughs) Those are all just stories I tell myself so I can be right or feel sorry for myself or feel vindicated, aren't they?

Yep.

Well then, how would you put it?

Let us show you what we see from our perspective. This will also give you a further insight into what you call co-creation as well as how your own thoughts and feelings create. But, before we start, we don't want to get into your story because that just keeps you charged and feeling harmed or self-righteous.

Awesome. I'm off the hook.

Not quite, but in a nutshell here is what happened: this relationship came together because it served both of your vibrational needs. You were vibrationally holding a fear of commitment. She was offering the fear of being abandoned. This gives you some insight into why the relationship always became strained when the topic of moving or furthering the commitment came into play.

In your own ways, you were both looking for drama, and in your own ways, you both wanted a way out of the drama. So, you who had a fear of intimacy could come forward and commit to someone who was not physically close, and she who had fears of being left, could commit to someone who was never really going to be there and therefore could never really leave.

You make it sound so simple and really there were some tough feelings there.

Drama.

I'm not saying I don't see that, I'm just saying it seems like an over simplification of the situation.

If you had cancer and were going to die, and someone came up to you and offered to heal you instantly, would you say "no thank you" and hold onto your cancer because you felt the need to honor all the suffering you had previously endured?

Hell no. I'd be thrilled.

Then be thrilled. So many times people hold onto their emotions because they feel like they have to honor their story. This is why we keep saying "let go of the story." The story here is: "It was complicated and I loved her, but she did this and I did this and woe is me, Love hurts!" Let that go. Love doesn't hurt, only your story makes it hurt. Let it go.

I can actually feel myself holding onto it when you put it like that. It's like you've told me exactly what created the relationship, I can see it, but I don't want to give up the picture of how I wanted it to look.

And by holding that picture, you are just giving yourself cause for not only more grief, but from preventing everything you do want in regards to love from coming forth. (Pause) Just take your own judgment out of the equation for a moment, and we'll finish explaining.

Okay. I can do that.

Good. Now, at some point, the vibrations in the relationship changed.

Yeah. It was when I started thinking about moving so that we could be together on a more permanent basis.

Nice try. You weren't moving to be with her. You were moving to suffer with her, because you held a belief at that time that said "in order to be loved, I must suffer, and when I suffer, I am loved."

Whoa.

Don't judge it or be afraid of it; it's only a belief.

So I was saying in effect, "I'll give up everything I want to do for you." You realize that a lot of people right now think that sacrifice is the ultimate expression of love.

We know. This is yet another thing we would like to make known: Self-Love is the greatest expression of love.

Now, through this experience, you actually began to embrace love and the idea of being loved. You began to shift and release. You began to expand. However, you can see quite clearly

148

how a belief in suffering in order to be loved would manifest as a fear of intimacy, can you not?

Sure. If I think I'm going to suffer if I love or am loved, and I don't want to suffer, then I could be using it as an excuse not to love or be intimate.

So, you shifted your vibration and came forward and said, "I want to experience love." Even though you still had a belief in suffering for love, your desire was so strong that it was now possible to push through that limitation, and your thoughts began to change—which began to change the outer creation. What's a better set up than this for what you created? If the glue that held the romantic entanglement together has now been altered, what happens? You were co-creating a relationship founded upon your fear of intimacy and her fear of abandonment. You left your fear of intimacy enough to where you were in a place of commitment. In your willingness to move and actually be present, she plugged into her beliefs about abandonment. Before, you were safe because you could not leave living far away. Now, you would be in a place to leave. Discord, discord, discord.

In actuality what has happened is you have both vibrated out of alignment with each other, which is not a good or bad thing. It just is. It may feel bad, but look at the how and the why. It only feels bad because you won't consciously move beyond the drama. You asked to experience love, which includes loving who you are, and who you are loves what you do and where you live. You

149

were in a co-created relationship based on your vibrations. When the vibrations change, so does the relationship. So you see you were actually being moved to the place you were asking to be moved into and could have trusted that. You were being moved into the ready acceptance of love, but you were moved there in a way that you created and allowed based on your own beliefs and vibrational offerings. So, the Universe knows exactly what you want, and it will ALWAYS keep trying to deliver it. All you have to do is allow. Allow by giving up expectations and "how it should look." Allow by releasing and letting go of the drama. And, we'll add this: it may wind up looking exactly the same as you had envisioned, and you may still choose the experience and potentiality of being with her, but you may not have been in the place vibrationally where you could have received and manifested that potential until you gave it over.

Gave it over?

Let it go. Said, "Here, Source. I trust you so much, that I'm going to get out of my own way."

Okay. You've mentioned the word "drama" a few times in this chapter. You also mentioned something about true feelings or emotions. Can we talk about that?

Absolutely. One of the ways you remain in places you consciously don't think you want to remain is by holding on to the drama. For example, one might say, "I can't believe my partner cheated on me" - making it all about the other person and creating within you a sense of victimization - or "I can't believe _____." fill in the blank. By really looking at creation and the energy and beliefs that create everything, you have to let blame go. You begin to see how everything comes into being and that everything comes into being for a reason, and that reason is that you created it. Every experience you have ever had came about because it matched the vibrations you were offering. You can see that even in the case of the abovementioned breakup, everything came together based on your vibration.

I can see that, but how does that play into "real" emotion or feelings?

Well, as we said earlier, "Your thoughts form the waves that guide your consciousness into the potentiality of your creation. The waves then form the frequencies, which form the vibrations, which form the frequencies, etc. which creates or brings in the outer experience." Your thoughts come from your Source. Your feelings come from the waves that are formed from those thoughts. If judgment is present, as it has been, there is emotional discord in the vibrations. This discord has confusingly been mistaken for thought. In other words, your ego has said, "This is what I think" and you have taken it for fact that the ego or the "I" is in fact you.

Isn't it?

In part, but what we are now asking is for you to move into the part of you that no longer separates from Source. In other words, to get back to who you really are, you have to go beyond the thoughts and examine the thinker. Who is thinking these thoughts and why? The simple answer here is the ego. You have given your power away to thoughts that were created initially from a judgment and these thoughts have become your standard point of creation - just as the ego or thinker has become the definition of who you think you are. This type of pattern can keep your creation in a loop because you are trying to solve a problem at the same level or with the same mind that created it.

So it's like the idea of creation vs re-creation again. If I define myself as my ego - or the separate part of me that doesn't know it is Source--I will continue to recreate based on the beliefs and energies that formed that ego in the first place.

Yes, *and* what we are bringing up now is more about a false sense of self. Using the phrase, "I think, Therefore I am," you can see the fallacy. You think you are the thinker, and that the thinker is what gives you an identity and existence. In reality, you are Source, hence you are able to offer thought. If you offer a thought in regard to what you are, that thought - whether characterized by you as good or bad - becomes a judgment. That judgment then elicits a feeling. So there has been discord between the true Self and what the thoughts perceive of as the self, or the ego.

So, the "me" doing the thinking is Source?

Yes, but in your individualized state. We'll use the metaphor of channels - judgment can cause the closing or circumventing of certain thought channels. It can cause feelings to not truly be developed or discovered. Most people "think" into a feeling or "feel" into a thought. In other words, you have a feeling, and you put words and emotions to it. Or, you have a thought, but you get a feeling about it - you give it power with your emotions. What we would ask that all consciousness do is to feel into the feeling and discover if it is truly a feeling or a thought. If you wish to experience Source as pure love, get rid of all of your thoughts about pure love and "feel" into it. Go as far as you can go, and then look to see what thoughts are present. Remove the thoughts and feel some more. Eventually, you will feel good and the only thought that will come is "I feel good." The thoughts and feelings will align in love and oh what a powerful creator you are when that happens. It is the nature of man to be happy. It might not seem that way, but that is because you have allowed a judgment to bypass a true feeling.

I think I get it, but that seems like a pretty big statement. We've talked about new thought, and it seems to me that this may just be one.

Indeed. In fact, new thought is what you might term entering the mind of Source.

I like that.

The only judgment present is the judgment you create. At your most expanded level, you are one with Source; therefore there is no judgment, only bliss.

Wow. I was just relating that to the earlier belief that I have to suffer for love.

Yes. So you see, if the consciousness as a whole is vibrating with a belief that it must suffer or sacrifice to be loved, or it must earn love, you could see where it might have a hard time trusting Source and trusting love.

And this ultimately comes down to trusting ourselves.

Correct. So, on behalf of all consciousness . . .

I am Self-Love.

You see, before, the drama gave you an out. It kept you safe from having to move into trust and love because the consistently held belief was that love was not safe. Now, you are free to choose, and as you begin to trust and watch the unfolding of your own creation, you will begin to notice Source constantly speaking to you.

Through synchronicity?

Yes, you would see it as that. In fact, you are really seeing your thoughts mirrored back to you from your physical creation. As your inner being unfolds, you will notice your outer expression mirroring back to you your own thoughts. This is how creation always works, but "synchronicity" is a word you have given to explain what happens when you consciously experience your creation at play.

Well, can you give me an example of something that most people would call "synchronistic."

Sure. You may be experiencing a situation in your life—say with regards to a relationship—that you would like to change. You ask Source to help you find a solution. Immediately, you go back to business, but a few minutes later, you turn on the T.V. and see an author talking about their new book, *All You Will Ever Need to know About Relationships.* That is Source Answering. To take it further, it might not "click" right away, but a few days later, you notice someone at a bookstore sitting down with a coffee reading the same book. You think, "Oh. That's the book I just saw on T.V. Maybe I should buy it."

This process is always occurring. The difference is, once you begin to look out at the world through the eyes of trust and as you allow yourself to step into your own power, you will begin to notice it everywhere. What you would call "synchronicity," we would call an active perception of Self-creation.

Can you give me another example?

Certainly. Here are a few:

1. Three people may recommend the same book to you within two weeks.
2. You may see a T.V. show and think of the location, "I'd love to go there," and a few days later you find yourself in a place very similar to the location on T.V.
3. You may be thinking about someone you haven't spoken to in years, and later you may get an e-mail or phone call from them.

Sometimes it can be instantaneous. You had the experience a few nights ago of wanting to go to a certain restaurant. Not five minutes after having that thought, a friend called you up and asked if you'd like to go eat there. Most people only call events "synchronistic" when they manifest fast or when something happens that they were consciously thinking of; but in truth, every manifestation is synchronistic because the outer and inner world are always vibrationally in sync. Nothing in your world is "coincidence," and manifestation can come as fast as you can allow. Synchronicities may not be the final manifestation of what you have asked for, but they are most assuredly signposts that you are creating your reality and telling yourself that you are going in the right direction.

Again, you began writing this book at a time when your industry was slow. You asked, "What am I supposed to do now?" Everywhere you turned for the next two weeks, people were saying, "You should write a book." You began noticing authors on T.V. The Universe was literally going, "Hello! Over here!" You just have to know that when you ask, you will receive. After that, simply trust and allow. If you have a hard time with this, use the previously mentioned tools to check your energy and see where you are. Know with all of your being that what you have asked for will come once you are in alignment with it, and know that as you align, synchronicities will abound. Use these to validate your trusting the Universe, because the more you can trust yourself and your creation, the easier it will be to let go of the resistance and the stories of creation you have held on to and allow the new to come in. You will see your old beliefs about creation, i.e., "I must do this in order to accomplish this," or "First this, then that" dissipate. It will be a fresh start. You will begin creating from the place we wish to address next: the blank page.

Chapter Eleven
The Still Point or Blank Page

We've moved through fear of creation, into intention, and now we come to the place we'll call, "the blank page." In the past, many of you have been able to move through certain fears and to align your energy and decide to do or accomplish certain tasks. At this point, you've had another choice to make - and many of you did not even know this was a choice or that it was with regard to your story. Most of what you have called creation has in actuality been a re-creation of energies, of scenarios, and a re-creation of patterns. These have come about because you have been "creating" from expectation. You have been "creating" from the totality of past experiences. We have come forward today to tell you that just as you can only create in the moment of now, so too can you only create something new from the place of the blank page. It is known to some as the void, or that place from whence creation comes. In terms of energy, it's also known as the zero point.

In physics, zero-point energy is the ground state of any system.

Yes, the neutral state of energy. Take this for example: if "I want it" is a positive charge, and "I don't want it" is a negative charge (not that such charges exist as positive and negative, but we are using these attributes to represent perceived polarities within the energy), the zero point would be the place where these two come together in absolute stillness. From this stillness arise the limitless possibilities of creation.

By bringing in your story, or who you perceive yourself to be, you limit creation. You are saying "I want this thing," yet you are bringing in definitions, judgments, and beliefs which say to the Universe, "It has to be this shape, size, color, and fit exactly within these parameters, or I can't receive it no matter how hard you try to deliver it." It is a shame to come this far only to not receive because you haven't let go of conditions based purely on stories.

This reminds me of a story I once heard about poachers using traps to catch monkeys. The monkey would reach in to grab the food, and their hand would get caught. If the monkey just let go, his hand would have slipped right out and he would have been free.

Yep. People hold on to their stories because like what was trapping the monkey, it's their food. They believe they will cease to exist without them. Therefore, they cling to the very thing that is keeping you from their freedom.

And we can all release our stories by claiming Self-Love?

Yes. However, we would like to suggest that before you employ this claim, you make the decision to move forward and just let your stories go. You must ultimately decide. Once you have made the decision, your energy will move into the next phase.

Can you give me an example of creating from a blank page as opposed to re-creating from a story?

Yes, if you will let the energy in. Your headache is a form of resistance. Claim Self-Love.

I am Self-Love.

(Long pause) I felt it go.

It didn't "go" as in evaporate. It returned to that which you are, pure Source Energy. It is important for us to make this distinction because we do not want you to think that your energy "goes" away. You are Source, constantly drawing from Source. Now for your example: Think of your creation like building a car. We know you do not know anything about building cars, but you know some of the parts that go into its creation. If you were told to build one, what would you do?

Well, I'd start out by reading about car assembly and viewing blueprints.

Yes. That would be one avenue of creation. What next?

Eventually, I'd have to start ordering parts, right?

Right. Now these parts are symbols of your story. The outside of your car may look different from others, but under the hood, there will always be certain basic parts. Thus has been the history of human creation to this point. You have created many different models, but you have been working from the same basic designs using the same parts. In this case, maybe you came into this life with certain parts, and maybe you picked others up along the way. Regardless, these parts have gone into making everything you perceive to be you, or your story.

The parts then are my beliefs, judgments, ideas, etc?

Yes, and more. As an example, we would like to use the image of a needle. You've heard it said that, "It is harder for a camel to pass through the eye of a needle than it is for a rich man to enter the kingdom." Well duh! A rich man has more stuff than a poor man. A poor man can say, "I have nothing, therefore I surrender everything." The poor man has no story other than his being poor, and if he can give up this story, he will enter into the kingdom—which, as we have mentioned, is within each of you. The rich man has many things and aspects of himself which he is attached to. He says, "I cannot let go of everything, for if I do, I will be as poor as the poor man." His attachments have kept him from surrendering to the blank page from which creation is born, i.e., you without your story.

Now, we will provide another example because we do not wish to leave you with the idea that material possessions are a hindrance. They are merely physical manifestations you have called forth from your desire for experience.

Emotionally, you may say I am an unhappy person. I am depressed. We would say, well, why are you depressed? You may answer in several ways.

1. You might claim not to know.

2. You might list the things in life you think have made you unhappy, or

3. You might say, "I have a chemical imbalance."

None of these answers would be incorrect, but they would all be aspects or parts with regard to your story of the depression. Could you let these things go? Can you see that none of them define who you are? They are just your experiences. You cannot move through the eye of the needle to the blank page, because your bag carrying your depression is too filled. Can you let go of the story? We are not telling you, say you are not depressed, and you will not be. We are saying, how has depression come to define you? How has your story kept you from what you wish to experience?

Well, I did have a friend tell me that he had a cold and was tired of coughing and sneezing all day, so he sat down and repeated the mantra, "I Am Perfect Health" for twenty minutes, and it all just stopped.

Indeed, he dropped one story and claimed another without the previous "parts." But, we are talking about a slightly bigger picture. We would say the largest story most in this plane have held is that of "I am not God. I am not the creator of my reality." A few have come here and released this story. Instead of adopting and spreading their message, institutions were set up to worship them. This is not to take away from the messengers in any way, for they are wonderful - they are you. This may be the most difficult story to release because for thousands upon thousands of years, there has been a belief in judgment and damnation. You see now yet another layer in which fear of creation plays a role, and here on a global scale.

When we release our fear of knowing we are all one creation and that we are in fact the directors and creators of this energy, we move into and through our intention of remembering our oneness with all, and we come to the point of the blank page. We release thousands of years of consciousness that has said "You are not God." We refresh our own energy. We're now able to move forward in creating the knowing that we are One and that we are the creators of our own reality without the baggage of thinking we aren't. We're able to let go of everything that has come before, and we are able to fully enter the moment of now. We're able to release our attachment to everything, including outcomes, because as the blank page, all is well. We're truly in the moment of creation.

We're always in the moment of creation though, right?

Very good, but now, as the blank page, you are free to truly create—as opposed to re-create, for there is nothing *to* re-create. No more stories. Do you follow?

All the way to the blank page.

Welcome aboard! It's a wonderful thing to see the consciousness poised to do this. The potential is awe-inspiring.

So, what happens to the ego, which from my understanding is the conglomeration of our stories, individual and cultural?

It evolves. The "ego" has been given this magical, powerful status as "who I am." In reality, ego is not the Source of self. Self is the Source of self. Self exists as that larger version of the "you" that knows it is Source. That part knows who you are, and that part knows it can never die. The ego doesn't; yet your ego is not something to be feared. You have come here to experience yourself as an individualized expression of

Source energy. Even if you've chosen to remember who you are, you wouldn't be able to have that experience had you not had your ego. Your ego has received a bad rap. It's been your identity, and it's feared losing its grip, yet you may say to your ego - your sense of identity - "You will not die. You will evolve."

Your ego is the total summation of your stories and the picture of what those stories create. It houses all that you think you are, yet you are so much more, and as you learn this, your ego loses its grip. There will be a shift in your consciousness, and your ego will not have the hold it once had over you. Know that your ego is also your energy. It is yours to change.

Interestingly enough, it's your ego that says "No. This isn't true. I'll die!" There is no "I" that can die, and energetically, you know this. It's a game you play with yourself. Know you're safe.

With regard to war, there is most often a build-up of energies that explode or collide. When consciousness can lose its attachment to war, there will be no more war. What better way to lose attachment to war than by just losing it?

Trust that when you can know you are your own creator, you will be unaffected. The earth may fall all around you, yet you will be unmoved, as the saying goes. At this point we wish to claim Self-Love around everything we've discussed so far, on behalf of all consciousness. If there are no more questions, we will proceed with the next chapter.

Let's do it.

Chapter Twelve

The Unification of Body and Spirit

Once you've moved into the blank page - the still point – it becomes possible to truly unify the frequencies of body and spirit.

The body is the physical manifestation of spirit. The belief has been held on this plane that the body is simply a vessel in which the spirit dwells. This is incorrect, as without the spirit there would be no body, which is the vessel you have created to experience the physical manifestation of spirit.

Why not include the mind?

The mind has been thought of as separate from the spirit. It's not. Humanity has also incorrectly ascribed the mind as a function of the brain.

Yeah, I know a few brainy people who are mindless.

Cute, but that's the opposite of what we mean. Your brain is a mechanism of function. It performs regulatory tasks within the body, and allows communication from within the body. However, thought does not originate in your physical body. You have this idea that your mind is a collection of electrical impulses within the brain. Your mind is not housed in your brain and neither are you. The brain works much like that of a telephone operator; it routes the energy to the places you direct it. What you think of as mind exists and extends far beyond the physical and exists within the field.

You mentioned that term earlier. What exactly is the field?

As you know it, it is a place of all possibility. As science knows it, it is the interconnectedness of all that is.

I was hoping for something less New Age sounding.

All right. Your atmosphere is one of the best ways to illustrate what the field actually is. Think of thoughts as wind currents and the field as the air through which they blow. You can't really separate wind from air, thus you can't separate thought from the field. You can, however, isolate them—meaning that you can have cross currents, opposing currents, tornados, etc.

And in this example, a tornado might be rage or anger?

It could be any dominating thought in your atmosphere. It does not have to be viewed as a negative thing. However, if you are holding two opposing forces in the same field, you will create pressure—this is what is creating the stress you are currently feeling. It feels to you as if your body is stressed out, but the body is just a physical manifestation of Spirit. Somewhere in your field, you are holding opposing energies.

Think of these energies as magnets. The harder you try and pull them together, the more they resist.

Just thinking about it stresses me out. .

Then claim Self-Love.

I am Self Love.

Look at the difference in what you have written.

You hyphenated "Self" and "Love."

Because this is the frequency which brings both together.

Okay, well, I'd like you to finish explaining the field concept, and also look at these opposing beliefs and how or where they fit in.

Very well. The field is literally "the field" on which all energy plays in your world. It also expands into the sleep state and bridges dimensions, time, and space. It connects everything. For example, when one has what is termed "past life" recall, they are simply accessing a now moment from within the field. The perception is that said moment exists in another time or space, but within the field, all exists. Remember our clock metaphor. It is only perspective that causes this illusion of "other" or "separate." Everything exists in the here and now. Pre-cognitive dreams fall into the same category of "recall." The future is not a set event and one is always free to choose, yet all outcomes are present and open. If one "sees the future," they have simply looked out into the field and viewed a now moment in non-linear time.

What do you mean "non-linear time?"

We use that expression because it is the best way for you to begin processing that there is no time. You experience time as accumulated momentum; in other words, now exists because something came before. There is a cause and effect. Your memory stores every single moment, so there appears to be a linear flow to existence. The perception rendered is that your now is the direct result of past events. In correlation, "waiting" is simply an extension of this belief. You believe that "now" is the sum of your existence, therefore any future experience must be built towards. Time then becomes an anticipatory experience either resulting from or building towards another moment. In truth, the only moment that exists is the moment of now. The illusion of time requires a progression and a flow (also a story). If you can start to see that every moment you have ever experienced is simply a now moment, then your concept of time begins to unravel and you can begin to understand the vastness of existence and how everything is truly happening in the moment of now.

And this particular "time or space" is just a perception?

Correct. Your perception is that moments accumulate because this is how your memory works. This can be shown to be false by anyone who has ever had a precognitive experience. How is it possible to remember something before it has happened? It's not.

That's pretty wild. That explains time, but what about space?

Last night, you thought of your friend and sent her a text message. At the exact same time you pressed send, you received a message from her. You had not spoken in a while. It was rather late. There was no "real" explanation other than coincidence. As you now know, there is no coincidence. What actually occurred was much like an eel giving off electricity in water. Or we could also use the example of a dolphin using sonar. You both "picked up" on the same thought floating in the field. Who thought of who first is of no consequence because again, time and space are the result of your individual perception. Source knows no time or space because it perceives the whole.

Relate that to the field.

Time is the perception of separation between moments. Space is the physical manifestation of the same principal. To you, space exists as the places in between objects. Yet, physical reality is just as much an illusion as time. No object is actually "solid." Therefore "space" exists everywhere, and if space is all there is, there can be no physical objects to separate from each other. Ergo, all are one.

So the field is where everything unifies?

Yes. You know that your immediate environment is mostly water: your planet is covered in water, and your body is mostly water. Think of those things as metaphors for the larger whole of creation. All of this water must serve some purpose, right? Well, it does. It conducts. It is the literal manifestation of the communicative properties of the field.

Whoa - Big words. I'm not that brainy. Bring it home for me.

Just as electricity is conducted through physical water, so too does mind move through atmosphere. The field in this metaphor is water, and mind is electricity. Is that clear?

Yes. I got that.

So, let's get back to the concept of opposing currents. Your beliefs and judgments are at play within the field of your physical body—which is again, an expansion of spirit: as above, so below.

So by holding conflicting beliefs about myself, I'm creating tension in my field, a sort of stress storm as it were?

Yes. This is why we asked you to claim Self-Love. When everything is unified, there is a great calm. This is a very real process that requires intense honesty, so on behalf of all of creation, let us claim Self-Love together.

I am Self-Love. (Pause) What do you mean intense honesty?

We simply mean that you must be willing to look at your thoughts and honestly know that you are the creator of that thought. This brings up another question?

Yes. What about mass consciousness? I mean, I think we've all had the experience, where we've been going along, and all of a sudden we don't feel so great, and we realize that someone else's crappy energy has started to affect us. I know that we are the creators and that on some level we would have had to allow that in as we discussed earlier, but how does that work with regard to the concept of the field?

Excellent. Your energy picks vibration up before your brain registers reaction. As we have said, the brain has a place within the relay system, but it is not *the* system itself as it has been claimed. Therefore, when this happens, you are literally absorbing another person's charged atmosphere. Their field is "rubbing off" on yours. That is why so much emphasis is being placed on "conscious" living right now. If you are not consciously creating your life, you may fall prey to that "one bad apple spoils the bunch" category. It would be like a fish entering the proximity of an eel that electrocutes it. You are not necessarily a bad apple, but you're allowing yourself to be influenced and affected by one.

The poor mindless fish...

No. You are looking at the situation and saying that the eel killed the fish. The fish was there by choice, was he not?

Well, remember those "ass holes" from chapter 4—the ones who seem to get everything they want at the expense of others? I guess I'd say this is an example of an "ass hole" eel.

(Pause) Right. I am Self-Love. (Pause) So where does that leave us?

When the mind and spirit come together from the blank page, ego is transcended. Self and self merge. This removes all separation and thus resistance, judgment, and victimization as well. In this place you literally see what the ego has seen, yet you see beyond and through it. The totality of who you are now shifts—thus the evolving sense of Self. Again, the ego is transcended in its current form, but it evolves with the energy. By moving through the fear of creation frequency, into and through the frequency of intention, into the frequency of the blank page, then into and through the frequency of the unification of mind and spirit, you allow divine love to come in, and this is what we mean by spirit. We mean that which you truly are: Source. You are united with Source. The frequency of your physical body changes in that you have unlocked your potential to allow Source to unify with your physical being. The possibility to do that which you would perceive as evil cannot exist in this uniting because true Spirit is love.

Was that your way of saying that I can't use Self-Love for evil ... even if I wanted to?

Again, that which you call "evil" is a perception which comes from your limited perception of reality. If you knew truly that there was only self-creatorship at work in all things, even in situations which are unspeakable violations to you, you would see that there are no advantages or liberties taken. The eel is no more or less a self-creating form than the fish. We understand that this concept bothers you. We wish you to move through this resistance. By not recognizing the creation of others, you are limiting your own. You are saying, "Yes. I believe I create, except in circumstances where the outcome is less than desirable."

I can see this, and yet it makes me angry when I think about it.

Why? Does it make you angry to take total responsibility for your creation?

Yes. I guess it does.

Claim Self-Love around this. Know your own creation. We understand how this seems like an undesirable statement to you, and yet creation cannot come forward—consciousness cannot expand into knowing its own nature—if it is able to claim itself as a victim. There are no victims. We are not saying that if something you deem as wrong or bad happens to you that you are to blame. We are not speaking of blame. We are speaking of responsibility. It is your responsibility to release blame, and recognize that whether consciously or not, you have created the situation. We've spoken to you of ways in which you may unconsciously create; therefore, we are not saying the person who is seemingly wronged by another consciously set out to create the situation, but through their belief systems and fears the situation was created by them. The situation was created to serve as a physical mirror to what they were holding energetically. Again, if someone cured you of cancer, you would rejoice because you would no longer be in the physical experience of having cancer. Why then do you continue to hold physical experience beyond its actual moment of experience? You can release anger or hatred or blame or judgment just as easily as you can release the story of a sickness you have healed from.

Please understand, we are not saying that abusers or breakers of the law should not be punished. We are suggesting, however, that their punishments are of their own creation. We are not saying go out and commit crimes knowing that whomever you burglarize will have created you burglarizing them. Energy does not judge. It honors itself.

Whoa. What does that mean?

It means that there is no random occurrence. (Pause) You will have a better understanding of these principles once we explain the last frequency.

Is that when I get my frequency mileage?

Yes, enough to get you into the ionosphere, we hope.

Chapter Thirteen

The Expansion of Consciousness

You see, in a consciousness where expansion was resisted, you could not expand into an understanding of the lessons we are here to teach. This is the last frequency we address, as without it, you could not expand to match your desires. On one level, you must expand your consciousness to know that you are your creator, and on another, you must expand your consciousness to include that which you have called forth.

It's all very multi-level, huh?

Vast and brilliant.

We've asked that when you claim Self-Love, you claim it on behalf of all energy because as consciousness expands, new frequencies are encompassed, new vibrations are chosen for all. Self-Love grows as you grow. It is self-sustaining and ever evolving - just as you are - and it evolves on all levels.

So as consciousness expands, the Love frequency expands?

Yes, and across the entire field – which also expands.

Can we talk a little about the expansion of consciousness? We've covered vibrations and waves and potentials, and I guess my question is, isn't that expansion too?

Yes, it is, but it's not the expansion of consciousness, which is what allows for the expansion of vibrations and frequencies. It allows a more vast potential to be explored.

What we mean when we speak of the frequency of the expansion of consciousness is the allowance for new thought and the allowance of new ideas.

Mathematically speaking, the sequence of these frequencies equals creation. It's the blueprint for the beginning.

As in the Biblical, "In the beginning?"

That's the One. These frequencies bring your energy into the Alpha, or the beginning stage, for the manifestation of your desire.

So, they are equivalent?

Yes, the creation of the Universe and the manifestation of a new car is the same process, the former on a more expanded scale.

So no matter what I want, all I have to do is claim Self-Love?

Yes. You must choose, and the direction of divine love will do the rest. Within this love vibration are the frequencies which create the vibrations of manifestation.

So, what now? I mean, what comes next?

Whatever you want: a new car, a new relationship, or perhaps the realization of your God Self. It's a wide-open world from which to create.

It's a wide open everything. I mean, I don't even have the same definition of the world that I had just a few short months ago. Heck, I don't even have the same definition that I had a few moments ago.

Good. Your story is changing. Now, we've spoken to you about the origin of all things - You. We've explained how your reality is created, and we've given you the steps for the creation of divine love and manifestation.

Moving through the fear of creation, and then into and through intention, the still point/blank page, the unification of body and spirit, through the expansion of consciousness, we complete the formula with the allowance of Self-Love. We create ourselves as divine love. We create ourselves as creator.

Knowing that, we wish to ask the question of your consciousness, "Could everything be all right?"

Of course it could.

Could it? If everything were right in your life, how would that make you feel? Would you be okay with your life becoming all that you desire it to be?

Oh, I get it.

Yes?

No, I was just saying ... You know, I'd like for my answer to be "Yes." I really would.

Here comes that word you like to use . . .

But...

Why the "But?" Why can't you just have everything you say you'd like?

Because part of me thinks that I wouldn't know what to do with myself if I were suddenly loved beyond measure, if I were suddenly rich beyond my wildest dreams.

The part of you that "thinks," huh? What about the part of you that feels?

Well, I <u>feel</u> a little anxious about the prospect of being totally free. I have to be honest.

So, you're... afraid? Possibly of being your own creator? Hmm. Does that sound familiar?

Oh. Right. I am Self-Love.

Indeed. Feel into your thoughts. Some of you (including you, Mr. Hewett) may find that you're releasing little parts. Self-Love will cover all the bases, but you have to be willing to know that, to trust that. You have to be willing to give up. "Let go and let God," remember that? We'll keep saying it until we all truly get it. Let go. You're not giving over to something outside of you. You're giving over to YOU. You're giving up all of your bullshit . . .

Did you just swear? You've been hanging out with me for too long.

(Laughs) Forever... literally. That's all you have to do, though: just let go. Be willing to change. Allow. If you get into your head, make the conscious choice to move into your heart. That's all you have to do. Tune in. Literally. Tune in to the vibrations of your heart - your true heart - which is love, and let your heart create your world. Let the vibrations of love pour out into your creation. It will be easier and more glorious than you ever allowed your mind to imagine.

So, "Could it be all right? Can I be happy in a drama-free life?"

These are questions to ask yourself, because if you require resistance in order to change, you will experience resistance. If you require suffering to change, change will require suffering. We ask that you look at these pathways and that you decide, that you choose, to let them go. They are your story only as long as you allow them to be. Let your story of creation go. Let go of that which you think you must do. You must do nothing.

Other than claim Self-Love, right?

In truth, you must do nothing to be God. You are Source Energy no matter what you do. Self-Love will just allow you to let go. It will allow you to let in your creation. Ultimately, you direct. That is all. There have been so many layers of impediments that the vast majority of people

185

have not been able to get clear vibrationally about whom and what they truly are. Don't get us wrong, everyone knows this on some level. They remember, but they hide this memory from themselves. They don't allow themselves to know who and what they are, and therefore they devise other identities and form new beliefs, which will perpetuate those selves. True Divine Self-Love will allow you to let go of these beliefs and create your own unfolding from a more conscious perspective.

Self-Love will change your consciousness. It will expand not just your desires, but your entire being. As you expand, so we expand. Your creation will never end—just as your world will never end. Sure, there are books and religious texts that seem to imply a cataclysmic ending, but...

It's like the lyrics to "Closing Time." *"Every new beginning comes from some other beginning's end," huh?*

Yes. Look at what's going on currently in America. Everyone thinks the sky is falling. And guess what? As you believe, so shall it be. The media mirrors back to you the social consciousness, the social consciousness then acts accordingly. The media then reports on this new downturn, and the cycle continues ever downward. The only question you really have to ask yourself is, "What do you want?"

Look at it this way - and we are speaking to everyone who is reading these words right now, because your energy is just as much a part of this experience as any "other" - How do you qualify your energy? What do you focus on?

You can't be drawn in anywhere, because you are the only presence acting everywhere. You create your world—not the banks with their hedge funds, not Wall Street with their junk bonds, not the media. Love the people who are choosing to experience separation right now, but do not dwell there with them. Heal whatever poses the illusion of being broken within yourself—for if you are in reaction to a situation, your energy is still dancing in the drama.

Can you go over that one more time? Like, if someone does something that pisses me off, you're saying that I'm a co-creator of whatever that is?

Yes. Again, this is not about judgment or blame or any of those beliefs. It's simply about moving out of a "polarizing" energy. Consciousness is moving into and beyond what we have previously called "convergent" energy. We'll discuss this in a moment, but we would like for you to simply see that any time a reaction is present, there is a certain kind of energy behind that reaction. It's not wrong or right to have or not have a reaction, but if you stay plugged in—for example: You say you want justice and equality for all minorities. There is a slight but critical difference between creating an experience wherein everyone is equal and a situation wherein you seek out injustice.

It's not wrong to want to "right" an injustice; however, by seeking out injustice, you will perpetuate the energy that creates injustice.

Okay. You just gave me another one of those "Say what?" explanations that people are going to keep asking me about.

Well, that fear should tell you right there that you still carry what you would term "an unbalanced charge" around the concept of justice and even self-creation itself.

Wow. So, it really is that simple? If I knew with 100 percent of my being that everyone creates their own world, that question would not bother me?

You wouldn't even be asked it, we would imagine. Many people questioning you won't accept this answer anyway, and your doubt is a weakness they exploit to make them right.

And we know that to you, this looks like a very severe statement—AND—it only looks that way because of the stories you're carrying around and the perceptions those stories shade, maintain, and even help create.

You see, when you truly know peace, peace is all that surrounds you. When you truly know you create, the energy of your creation is all that surrounds you. It's not a scary thing at all. In fact, it should be quite liberating . . .

This kind of scares me.

You know the drill.

I claim Self-Love.

Well, also feel what it really feels like to love with no condition. Feel it. Feel what it is like to be totally free—and free in the sense that you are in love with everyone and everything and that love is mirrored back to you at all times in all ways. That is what Self-Love is. Now, you may from time to time come across an experience that you may wish to change, and all you have to do is change it. Don't judge it. Don't go into reaction. Don't fight with it—for all of those approaches only serve to create resistance or something to push against, and you're really only ever pushing against you.

Now, at this time, there are still a lot of people *choosing* to push against themselves. There are a lot of people choosing to clash and choosing to experience limitation. These people are in bondage to their conditioned thoughts and beliefs because they have chosen to be. If it is their desire to awaken to some other knowingness, they will do so. The choice is theirs, and it is neither right nor wrong. It is merely *their* creation, but it does not have to be yours.

Simply know that you are the creator of your world. If you find yourself in reaction to something, there is an inner reason. This inner reason is the same thing that caused it to show up in your life in the first place.

As above, so below?

189

Indeed. The outer is a reflection of the inner. Always—whether you are consciously aware of it or not. That's why we say "Just let go." Let go. Claim Self-Love, and let go of all of your stories—especially judgments.

Okay. Well, I think I'm moving through that one.

Know something else. Know what you want to know. Don't even know that you've moved through it because in that knowing, you are still carrying around the story of what you once knew. Know only what you want.

Now, we wish to further discuss these "convergent" energies.

We previously discussed "polarities," and we've shown you how everything is really one energy. The only thing that separates is perception - whether created via fear or judgment or something similar. We have discussed much of creation with you, but we've not yet discussed convergent energies, because up to this point, such energy was not able to exist on a large scale.

But, now it is?

Yes. Most definitely. You hear people talk of "new energy" all the time, and we have told you that all energy simply is. Source is. There is no "new" Source, only Source, and the expansion of Source.

Like the law of Conservation of Energy: nothing gained, nothing lost.

Yes. Now, convergent energies are energies which through your perspective come together to heal. They are what most people today would term "miracles" or the "presence of God." In fact, they are simply "The Isness" Of energy.

Wait. You said "to heal." To heal what?

To heal itself. It is the one-energy coming together free of separation. It is the remembrance and experience of the perfection that has always been.

Wow. That feels big.

Well, you can't get any bigger than everything.

No, I guess not.

Consciousness on this plane has been creating polarity in its mind for so long that it has forgotten that polarity is not real. Through Self-Love, through the balancing of these frequencies and vibrations, the energy is coming together in a massive way right now. The old perspective with the illusion of opposing forces is falling away. That is what is going on right now in your world. We said earlier that people think the sky is falling; well, in a way, it is. But it is only falling because there is something so much more wonderful to be seen. In a world of opposites, better would be in relation to worse. In the "new" energy, the energy is coming together or converging and healing itself. As the layers of your stories fall away, the energy begins to return to its natural state of blissful neutrality—and it is

191

becoming free to be whatever it wishes to be—which is whatever you direct. In a world where polarity was the dominant story, this could not be achieved because there would forever be a back-and-forth motion: good to bad, bad to good. These times are exciting. They do not have to be experienced as bad. Simply know what is going on: Everything is healing and coming into balance.

Okay, on the one hand, I can say something is neither good nor bad, it just is. But sometimes I feel myself wanting to cling to my sense of righteousness. But if I understand what you're saying, as long as there is righteousness, there will be unrighteousness?

Yes. The "polar opposite."

The two need each other in order to survive?

And to sustain the illusion of separateness. But, when you can just know peace, you are embracing your own love—the "Isness" of all that is—and these polarities cease to be.

Wow. You know, I'm thinking about this activist I ran into outside the local grocery store. As I was leaving, this woman asked me to sign her petition. I politely declined and walked on. She started yelling at me. "Do you want to live in a world where (fill in the blank) happens... We need to get those fuckers!"

With this explanation, it suddenly becomes very clear to me that she was a part of the very energy she was claiming she wanted to change, because she was focused on an adversarial us-them scenario.

Indeed.

So, when she can shift from "let's get the bastards" to "I choose love," she will not only see the change she wants, but be that change.

Yes. Just know that whatever you send your energy toward will grow. Remember the plant in "Little shop of Horrors?" Life works just like that. Whatever you feed, will grow.

Everything is one consciousness. You don't have to fight to push closed a door you are afraid to keep open. You simply have to know that you choose to create a new door, and only that which you create will shape your reality. Politics are tricky only if you believe they are. Yes, there are global shifts coming, but shift happens every day. What people are feeling right now is a collective panic. If you can hold on to your own balance, you will not only stay unshaken in the midst of the storm, but you will put peace and stability back into the one-energy which will begin to mirror it back, which will help create a sense of peace, which will continue to perpetuate and change the exterior conditions.

Kind of like inertia: things keep moving in one direction until a force acts upon them.

That's not a bad way to describe it. But we would say: it just is; it is whatever you decide to direct it to be.

To continue with consciousness, people tend to see two sides of consciousness: They see a sort of uniform totality of consciousness—of which we are all a part, and a singular totality, which would be the individualized experience of you. Another way to put this would be: within the one are the many, and within the many you will find the one. This can be demonstrated through what you perceive as the polarity of individuality, which is simply another fractal of duality consciousness within the one.

Fractal of duality? I feel like I'm in science class. What does that mean in everyday terms?

We used the example earlier of a picture that comes together to form a larger picture.

Oh, right. Like those movie posters where they take a bunch of tiny little pictures, and arrange them so that from far off, they make up an entirely new larger picture.

Not quite. The smaller pictures and the larger picture are both the same. Remember our conversation about holograms?

Oh, so in this case, each piece of the smaller image contains the whole of the larger image? Or, with regard to what you just said, we're all a part of the larger consciousness; everyone is Source energy?

Yes. Your belief is that "within the one, there are many." This is only true so far as you perceive it to be, like our earlier explanation about polarity. Can you see beyond the separation where you can know that all are one, and that the one is choosing an ever-growing multitude of possible experiences? You are one of those experiences, yet you are not separate at any time from any other. Creation is never-ending; it is always expanding, and so within the one there are many desires which are fulfilled in infinite ways—none better, worse, or separate from the other.

As you begin to move beyond your perception of polarity, it is possible that you will begin to feel emotions or feelings that are not entirely yours— at least what you would perceive as yours. What you are feeling is the luminous presence of fear within the collective consciousness, and the paradox here is that you are a part of that consciousness.

Therefore, that fear is in you, but it is not of you. It's not originating from your individualized being. We've spoken to you about creation and about the effects of energy and energy within energy and vibration within vibration. What we wish to explain is that while you are individual, you are an individual made manifest from a collective desire of all that you are—which is Source—and that there is never a separation from Source, only an infinite choice of direction made possible by your perceived separation.

Are you saying I'm screwed no matter what, and that I have to walk around feeling everyone else's crap?

Absolutely not. You are only "screwed," as you so colorfully put it, if you choose to be. We bring this up only because, as you move through your own energy and release those beliefs and ideas that no longer serve you, you may come to a point where there is nothing more to be released, yet you may still feel a certain emotion or feeling tugging away at you. What we are saying is that all you must do at that point is consciously choose whether or not to allow this feeling to be OF you.

Be in the world, not OF the world.

Right. Jesus knew exactly what he was talking about.

Being in the world, but not of it is a fine example. In one way, you have grown or expanded beyond your own energy, and therefore you are now feeling that greater YOU that is the collective. Now, that collective is being fed by the energies around you. In choosing to stay focused on love, and peace, and abundance, and whatever else it is that you wish to experience, you shift that larger collective of energy. You literally shift all of consciousness. The thing that was not of you that was making you feel uneasy will become smaller and smaller as less and less focus is cast upon it. (Not to complicate this explanation, but that thing which you felt was being felt for a reason—even if it was drawn to you through your desire to bring peace and balance.) So we are speaking of these matters knowing that they are the questions and answers held in positions of belief. Eventually, through direction of energy, release of limitation (all of which comes down to knowing), what was thought of as impossible by most, will be an acceptable norm. You will see the change on a massive scale.

This can best be illustrated through the example of the four-minute mile. It was thought an impossible feat by the collective until an individual came forward and said, "No, I can run the four-minute mile." When that individual ran the four-minute mile, it broke down that barrier for consciousness, and that concept then permeated the entirety of the consciousness and more individuals then achieved that goal. Now, what happened in this particular example, is that the desire was formed in the consciousness for something new, and it was plucked out by an individualized experience of that consciousness. It then manifested the experience that it wanted, which then announced to the rest of the consciousness that it was possible to do so, and the rest of the consciousness picked up that this desire could manifest, and thus actuated the experience of it. Now, this is often the case, where the idea will come from a singular source—in this case meaning the individualized experience—and the idea will have come forth from a desire. Now whether or not that desire is from an individual or from the collective does not matter, because they are one and the same at the level of truth. Once the desire has been put there, in the field of potentiality, that desire is manifested or unmanifested in a myriad of ways, which then propels the consciousness into expansion and growth through the realization of that potentiality. Thus is the evolution of thought. Thus is new thought. Thus is expansion.

So what do I do?

Claim Self-Love. "Less of me and more of Thee," only the "thee" here is your own Divine Source—The Divine Source of All. In claiming so, you turn your focus to all that you are and direct only Love to permeate your consciousness.

It's really all about a shift in consciousness. Look at the fear and speculation around "the end times." People have been afraid of "the end" on this plane since they first gained self awareness. It's never the end of time. Prophecies about the end times are all symbolic, but not of the destruction of the planet – but in a way destruction of the smaller, limited self. To this self, enlightenment looks like the end because it has to give up all of its control, greed, hunger for power. In actuality, the end is never the end; it is merely the end of "not knowing." It's the end of keeping yourself small. It is the beginning of conscious creation. It is the beginning of the new era - of expansion, of God... of You. The frequencies we have revealed will be a major catalyst in the evolution of consciousness.

Through the allowance of Self-Love, the consciousness will open up in such a way as to allow the convergent energies to radiate and stream forth in a known manner. In essence, mankind will be able to feel the love and being of all that he truly is. There is nothing to fear about the future, or any other "time" because again, what has been prophesied and feared by some as "the end" is simply a renewal: the renewal of your ability to know your Self. This will mark the expansion into all that is, and as you come forward for yourself, you crumble the walls that your fear has put up. As you speak your truth and come forward as all you are, the light that you are is able to fully move into this individualized place that you have come to be. This light then catches the eye of all those around you who do not yet remember who they are, yet are seeking to know. And as this light grows, so grows peace and safety, and harmony, tranquility, and love. We have said in all of this, that we may come back to love—that you may see love is truly the key.

Your thoughts sometimes tell you that conscious creation is a myth, that it is an idea, and what we have shown, is how everything you experience is a myth. Everything is an idea. Everything is potential. Choose the potential. Choose the outcome. Choose to move into that potential, and in that potential choose to actualize all that you want and trust. This is what is meant by "faith." Have the "faith"—faith meaning "to know." Know it is here already. Know it is until it is.

We wish you love.

Namaste.

Epilogue

A few days after finishing the last chapter of this book,
I found myself sitting on a mountaintop in beautiful Spanish Hills, California watching one of my best friends tie the knot. As she and her very soon-to-be husband stood smiling and laughing and looking into each other's eyes, the minister read a passage from first Corinthians:

"Love is patient, love is kind. It does not envy, it does not boast, it is not proud. It is not rude, it is not self-seeking, it is not easily angered, it keeps no record of wrongs. Love does not delight in evil, but rejoices with the truth. It always protects, always trusts, always hopes, always perseveres. Love never fails." 1 Corinthians 13:4

This is the very definition of the Universal Love available to us all. It doesn't matter what you call it. Source is always there for us, in whatever guise, always waiting patiently to give us what we've asked for at all levels of our being. It is abundant and contains all; therefore, it does not envy or judge. It exists to love and fulfill everyone, and in the end, that love always prevails. Joy is always the final outcome. The only real question is: Will you experience this alignment with love and abundance now while physically here in this time and space, or later? It's always up to you.

Enter Self-Love.

Everything is vibration. Everything is frequency: thoughts, beliefs, and emotions are just energy moving in accordance with our own direction and stories. What we are in this moment is always up to us.

One of the greatest gifts I've received from this material and my interface with Source is the knowledge that I can experience that pure, divine love in any moment that I choose. Within that context, I have to admit that when I first began writing this book, my story of "this moment" was something a little akin to one of those tube-shaped water balloon toys we all had as kids—the one that always slipped through your hands no matter how hard you tried to hold on. I perceived "now" as something unattainable; it was a tiny bull's eye that I felt destined to never hit. Therefore, everything I wanted was always some place in the past, or just out of reach sometime in the future.

Through Self-Love, I was able to give up that story, and in turn, experience the true, all-encompassing, vast moment of now.

I'll admit, sometimes the thought of "Why am I not *there* yet" still crosses my mind, and what I have to remember is: this is just another story. In reality, there is no "there." Everything is right here in the present moment, and it's when I can stay joyful and mindful and experience the present, that I experience that sense of newness and continuation of the present.

"Yes," I hear people say. "I'm in the present, and I'm in my joy, so why isn't this happening for me?"

Think of it this way: If your goal is to count to ten, and you begin counting, are you going to stop at the number five and ask, "Why am I not to ten yet?" Or, are you going to continue counting, knowing that you are heading in the right direction and will reach your goal? Let Source take care of the how's, who's, and why's. I like to think of Self-Love as a five-star hotel where all your needs are guaranteed to be met. There is nothing for you to do other than put down those bags, stay present, and enjoy it all.

Acknowledgments

I've had the privilege and honor of sharing my journey with some of the most remarkable people on the planet. I would like to take a moment and extend a special "thank you" to the following people:

Story Waters – You are amazing. Without your prodding, friendship, and encouragement, this book might still be an unmarked file on my computer. You are absolutely brilliant at what you do, and I thank you so much for sharing your gifts so bravely and freely with the world.

Dee Wallace – Where to begin? I think if I hadn't met you when I did, I'd be an unhappily divorced attorney suffering through an early mid-life crisis by now, lol. Thank you for your wonderful friendship. Shine as brightly as you possibly can!

Dr. Joe Vitale – Thank you for your continued support over the years. It's my turn to say it to you: "You're awesome."

Logan and Angela Wehling – My two best friends married each other. I love it. I couldn't have asked for two more wonderful people to have shared so many years of my life with. Talk about a journey. You two were pretty much on board through the entire process. As I sit here writing this, little Addie is almost a month and a half old, but it seems like just yesterday Logan was calling me up and saying, "I'm your best friend. If you're gonna dream about when anybody is going to have kids, it should be me!" … I've never been so happy to have been right; that little girl is gonna be so spoiled by her uncle Hewett. I love you guys.

Sheana Knighton – Thanks for all those Friday nights you stayed awake watching G-Dub and Num….zzzz…. I love every minute we get to spend together. You're my tadoodles, lil boops.

Mairead McAllister – Thank you for your healing work and for really helping me to ground my energy and center myself. Your light and love are a blessing to us all.

Mom and Dad – Don't think I wasn't about to mention you. I love you both enormously. As strange as it might be for a child to say this, I've watched you both mature and grow over the last thirty years, and I'm proud of both of you. You might not have always understood, but somewhere in there you knew you didn't have to.

Love was always enough. Thank you for that lesson.

PS. I know we like to kid around, but please don't come back and haunt each other through me.

Lastly, as strange as it sounds, I want to thank my dog. There's nothing like a sixty-eight pound lug of love to help open your heart. Thanks, **Pucker.**

About the Author

Jarrad Hewett is a spiritual author who seeks to empower others by sharing his personal humor and insight. Through his writing, he seeks to help others reconnect with their own inner guidance, wisdom, and peace.

Jarrad was born and raised in Oklahoma. He moved to Los Angeles in 2004 after graduating with honors from Oklahoma City University. He holds honorary doctorates in both divinity and metaphysics, and is an active alumni and supporter of the Lambda Chi Alpha fraternity.

In 2005, Jarrad began working as a voice actor and has since been the voice behind hundreds of television and radio commercials. He's also voiced major national and international campaigns for companies such as Coca-Cola, Toshiba, and The Ad Council of America.

For more information, please visit http://www.jarradhewett.com

To Love, To Life, To God

...and to the ever-expanding
Journey of Creation.

**Notes**

**Notes**

Notes

__Notes__

Notes